To

Ray —

Best Wishes

Harry F. Byrd

4/11/07

Double Trouble

Vignettes
From A Life of Politics and Newspapering

Harry F. Byrd Jr.

ACKNOWLEDGEMENTS

This book is the result of much help from Wynnona Kirk, Adrian O'Connor, Peter Yates, Karel McClellan, Penny Anderson and Pete Marovich.

ISBN-13: 978-0-9666870-1-9

ISBN-10: 0-9666870-1-9

Library of Congress Control Number: 2007900806

Printed by RR Donnelley & Sons Company
Harrisonburg, Virginia

TABLE OF CONTENTS

In memory of

Gretchen →

and our 48 happy years.

PREFACE

POLITICS AND NEWSPAPERS

I thought I should state promptly – and candidly – the not too desirable predicament I find myself. Call it a confession.

Almost all public opinion polls show that careers held in lowest esteem are politicians and/or newspapermen.

I, more than most, have cause for concern, for one simple reason: Throughout my adult life I have been both a politician and a newspaper editor. So, I am in double trouble.

I can't even depend on my colleagues in elected public office to sympathize with me because almost unanimously they regard newspaper people as the bottom of the barrel. And, conversely, my colleagues in the news media business view most politicians with suspicion. Neither has high regard for the other.

But over the years I have become accustomed to such a dismal evaluation.

So, this small book is written as vignettes of events and personalities, which to me are unforgettable.

Harry F. Byrd Jr.

Virginia/U.S. Senate
1948 - 1983

Newspaperman
1935 -

Rat Year
At Virginia Military Institute

※※※※

All freshmen at the Virginia Military Institute are called "Rats." Having matriculated and then entered the courtyard of that Lexington college in 1931 an upperclassman signaled me to stop and asked, "Do you know what you are?" I replied, "No." He said, "You are a Rat, the lowest form of humanity." I replied, "Yes sir."

I immediately began to contemplate as to how unpleasant the next nine months would be.

In those days, VMI barracks did not have hot water in the individual rooms. It required walking the Rat line to the end of the stoop to obtain hot water, simultaneously putting oneself at the whims of one or more upperclassmen.

I was age 16, the youngest in my class, and had just begun to shave. After a few weeks, I learned how dangerous was that short walk: "Go get my laundry" or "Come into my room," where I was told to bend over the table while one or more roommates would take a few whacks with a broom or bayonet.

After a few months, it was clear that I was being hazed more than anyone else in my class. It seemed to me that at least half of the upperclassmen wanted to say they whacked the governor's son.

My classmate acquiring the second highest number of hazing incidents was Arthur Ginsburg, a fat Jewish boy from Texas.

Ginsey and I developed a bond, and kept in contact, that lasted until his death, although he lived in Texas and Los Angeles. Such is the spirit of VMI.

While I was not happy about the hazing at the time, it didn't hurt me a bit. In looking back, I consider hazing an important part of the "Rat" system at a military college.

My "Rat" year made a lasting impression in several ways – one being permanent.

I began to avoid the hot-water trip by shaving in cold water; 75 years later, I still shave in cold water, as I did this morning.

My First Two Political Experiences

****

At age nine, I attended my first political event: My mother and father took me with them when they drove from Winchester across the Allegheny Mountains to Clarksburg, W. Va.

The purpose was to attend the acceptance speech of the newly nominated Democratic presidential candidate, John W. Davis. The 1924 Democratic national convention was held in New York City and became the longest, 103 ballots, in political history. It was nearly three weeks long.

The leading candidates were New York Gov. Alfred E. Smith; William G. McAdoo of California, secretary of the Treasury under President Wilson; Oscar W. Underwood, U. S. Senator from Alabama; and Virginia's Senator Carter Glass, who also had been Treasury secretary under President Wilson.

My father was the 37-year-old chairman of the Virginia Democratic Party and was in his third term as a state senator. He had been a delegate to the convention and a supporter of Senator Glass.

Radio was new in those days and I had listened to the convention proceedings on the smallest of the new invention, known as the "crystal set."

Before going to the convention, Chairman Byrd visited Senator Glass to pledge him support. In talking with Carter Glass, he also said that under no condition could he support Mr. McAdoo, and added that if Senator Glass thought my father's anti-McAdoo stance would be damaging to Glass' campaign for the nomination, that he (Byrd) would not go as a delegate. Senator Glass told him that it would not present a problem.

But as the balloting went on, the convention deadlocked and the delegates ran out of clothes, money, and patience. Senator Glass made a deal with Mr. McAdoo that he (Glass) and his supporters would support Mr. McAdoo for the nomination; if not successful, the Californian would then throw his support to the Virginian.

When this became known, young state Senator Byrd urged the delegates from Virginia to defy Senator Glass and refuse to cast their votes for McAdoo. He prevailed.

This infuriated Carter Glass, but he said he could not fault Byrd because Byrd had told him before the convention began that he would not support McAdoo.

Glass and Byrd became fast friends and Glass gave Byrd support the following year when Byrd sought the governorship.

My next experience with politics was the summer

of 1925, when my father became a candidate for governor of Virginia. My grandmother and my father's brother, Tom, took me to a political rally held in Purcellville. They had taken a room at a boarding house where both my grandfather, Richard E. Byrd, who was coming from Richmond, and my father, coming from a different part of the state, could change clothes.

When my grandfather arrived he was carrying a large package wrapped in newspaper. He was known to all as "Dick." I as a child called him "Big Dick." I said, "Big Dick, what do you have in that package?" He said, "Come with me and I'll show you."

When we got to the room he opened the package and there were two pistols. My grandfather told me that my father's life had been threatened and he, Big Dick, was prepared to shoot if necessary.

My grandmother, Uncle Tom, and myself were not permitted to sit on the stage with my father, as had been planned. It would put us in the line of fire.

As a result of this incident, so many years ago, today when people complain how bad politics are, I reply, "At least it's better than the pistol-carrying days of the 1920s."

While there was no shooting at the Purcellville rally, the man who made the threat to kill my father, did stab one of my father's supporters on Election Day. He was sent to prison.

Bringing Home The Mustard

✳✳✳✳

In 1929, Winston Churchill was a guest in our home at the Governor's Mansion in Richmond. We were told in advance that a distinguished British statesman was coming to visit. I, with my mother's older cousin, a leading lawyer who twice declined appointment to the Virginia Supreme Court, got our first glimpse of Mr. Churchill when he descended the staircase before dinner.

We were in our best clothes, and Mr. Churchill, thinking that my cousin was a member of the household staff, asked him to fetch a newspaper, two blocks away. On our return (I went with him) the lawyer was duly rewarded with a quarter, which he kept as a treasured possession all his life.

Winston Churchill was in Richmond to study the Civil War battlefields southeast of Richmond. His guide was Douglas Southall Freeman, editor of the Richmond News Leader and a noted historian.

During his visit, Mother and Father hosted a state dinner for Mr. Churchill and 20 local dignitaries. The main course was baked Virginia ham.

The guest of honor asked his hostess for mustard. My mother requested mustard from the kitchen, only to learn there was none in the house.

She apologized to Mr. Churchill and, seeking to pass it off lightly, said if he wished she would send someone to the store to fetch it. He said, "Yes, I would like that."

I was deemed too young to attend the dinner, so was dispatched to the store to bring home the mustard, while Mother slowed the dinner.

I often thought of this during World War II when it was Prime Minister Churchill, more than any individual, who did the most to rally the English people in their darkest hour.

He knew what he wanted, he persevered, and never gave up until his objective was achieved.

"I Am Going To Kill Gov. Byrd"

✳✳✳✳

In 1932, the Virginia delegates to the Democratic National Convention held in Chicago were supporting my father for the presidential nomination. My father had opened headquarters at Chicago's Congress Hotel. At age 17, I had completed one year of college at the Virginia Military Institute.

From Martinsburg, W. Va., I took an overnight train to Chicago, arriving on a Sunday morning. When I went to my father's headquarters at the Congress Hotel, a large tousled-haired man in a white suit was waving his arms and yelling, "Where's Governor Byrd, where's Governor Byrd? I'm going to kill him."

This shook me up quite a bit. After the big man was calmed down, and left, I was told he was Senator Huey Long of Louisiana.

It seems that Louisiana had sent two delegations to the convention – one pro-Long, the other anti-Long. My father, as a member of the credentials committee, had voted to seat the anti-Long group. This is what caused Huey's outburst.

My father, my uncle Admiral Richard E. Byrd, and I had a suite at the hotel and my job was to man the telephone. Two nights later, a caller asked to speak to

Governor Byrd, to whom I gave the telephone. When he completed the conversation, he told us it was Senator Long, who wanted my father to come to his room.

Dick, the Antarctic explorer, the first man to fly over the North Pole and then the South Pole, and in between the second person to fly the Atlantic Ocean, said, "Harry, you certainly are not going to his room. He threatened to kill you two days ago."

My father replied that he wasn't worried. Dick said that, unless his brother telephoned us within 10 minutes after reaching Senator Long's room, he would summon the security force to investigate. My father rang our phone to say there was no problem.

He was gone what my uncle and I thought was a very long time. We were on "pins and needles," so to speak. When my father finally returned, after what seemed like hours to Dick and me, he said the meeting went well; the Louisianian wanted to support the Virginian for vice president.

I learned that things can change quite fast in politics.

That 1932 convention was dominated by two candidates – Governor Franklin D. Roosevelt of New York, and his predecessor as governor, Alfred E. Smith. Roosevelt had the greater support.

The only hope of John Nance Garner of Texas, House Speaker, of Byrd of Virginia, of Governor Albert

C. Ritchie of Maryland, of Senator James A. Reed of Missouri, and of Ohio Governor George White, was to bring about a deadlock so Roosevelt could not get the required two-thirds vote of the convention. (The two-thirds rule has since been abolished).

On the first three ballots, it seemed that strategy might succeed. But the Roosevelt forces, after an all-night session, forced a recess before the fourth ballot could be taken, the recess being from 8 a.m. to 8 p.m.

When the convention reconvened, the chairman, Senator Walsh of Montana, recognized William G. McAdoo, a delegate from the State of California. California and Texas had been supporting John Nance Garner.

When Mr. McAdoo began walking from the floor to the podium, it was immediately apparent to most of the delegates that those two states would be shifting from Garner to Roosevelt.

During the 12-hour recess, James A. Farley, the Roosevelt campaign manager, made a deal by which the Texan, Mr. Garner, would receive the vice presidential nod and Mr. McAdoo would receive Roosevelt's support to be elected senator from California.

The ballgame was over. Franklin D. Roosevelt was nominated on the fourth ballot, and defeated incumbent President Herbert Hoover in November.

Eleanor Roosevelt's Anger

✳✳✳✳

In 1940 Europe was at war and Adolf Hitler's German war machine had overrun Poland, France, the Low Countries, Norway, Austria, and was preparing to take over England.

The United States was not in the war, but was sympathetic with England. Throughout America there were parties called "Bundles for Britain" to raise funds to help the British war effort.

One such party was held in Boyce, 10 miles from Winchester.

Elizabeth Whitney, the divorced wife of John Hay Whitney of New York, had as her guest at her home "Llangollen" near Upperville, Mr. and Mrs. Franklin D. Roosevelt Jr., son of the president and my contemporary.

Liz invited me to her home, but having to work I met her and the Roosevelts at the "Bundles for Britain" event in Boyce. It was a fine evening and raised a good bit of money for our friends across the sea.

When I went to work the next morning, the first thing I learned was that both Roosevelts were in Winchester Memorial Hospital as a result of an automobile accident on their way back from Boyce to

Upperville.

Learning of this, I went immediately to the hospital. I was in Frank's room trying to give him some comfort when his mother arrived. She was visibly in no mood to give her son sympathy. She was angry. Really angry.

Frank, being the attractive individual he was, and hoping to pass things off lightly, said, "Calm down, Mother, let me explain what happened."

(One of the large plants in Winchester is National Fruit Products Company and its brand name is "WHITE HOUSE.")

Frank said, "We were returning from the party, everything was going fine, when I saw a big sign in front of me. On the back of a truck, the sign in large letters read: 'White House.'

"I thought I was home, so I just ran into the 'White House.'"

His mother didn't appreciate that explanation.

I said to myself, "I best leave mother and son real fast."

Political Convention - 1940

****

Through the years, I attended seven national political conventions. While the 1932 Democratic convention is especially etched in my mind, it being my first, the most interesting was the 1940 Republican National Convention, held in Philadelphia the last week of June 1940.

At the beginning of that year, the leading candidates for the GOP's presidential nomination were Thomas E. Dewey, Governor of New York, and Robert A. Taft, U. S. Senator from Ohio.

Others with support were former President Herbert Hoover, Michigan Senator Arthur H. Vandenberg, and Governor Harold Stassen of Minnesota.

Herbert Hoover, the Depression-era president, had little support; Senator Vandenberg was impressive; Governor Stassen was the nation's youngest governor, having been elected to three two-year terms in 1936, 1938, and 1940. (He ran for president unsuccessfully every four years until 1996.)

It was not until March 1940 that a new name came under serious consideration – Wendell Willkie, president of a public utility company, Commonwealth and Southern. Willkie had been a life-long Democrat until 1939.

A major factor in bringing Mr. Willkie into prominence was Oren Root. Oren and I were at the University of Virginia together – I in my last year of college, and Oren's last in the university's law school.

We regularly met along with Murat Williams of Richmond and David Wright – later a law professor, but then a socialist arguing the desirability of social credit. In that quartet, we had two Democrats (Murat and me), a Republican, and a socialist.

We had lively political discussions once or twice a week, studying until 9 p.m., then meeting at a local pub to drink beer and argue political philosophy.

Oren became a partner in a top New York City law firm. It was from that venue that he became interested in Wendell Willkie. I covered convention proceedings for The Winchester Star and the Daily News-Record of Harrisonburg.

My previous association with Oren Root, and his enthusiasm for Willkie as a part of that candidate's inner circle, increased my interest in both the convention and the candidacy of Willkie, the non-politician.

While I covered press conferences held by Governor Dewey, Senator Taft, Senator Vandenberg, Harold Stassen, and others seeking the Republican nomination, it was Willkie I found to be the most interesting and spent the most time observing.

He had never been in public office or even sought it. But he had a way with people. He had what might be called the common touch.

On the first roll call, done alphabetically by states, the New York governor took the lead position, but faded fast in the next two ballots.

Willkie started slowly, but it soon became a race between him and Taft. Willkie's personality and campaign technique brought him the nomination. The galleries were stacked and "we want Willkie" calls were almost continuous.

1st ballot: Dewey 360; Willkie 105; Taft 189; Vandenberg 76

2nd: Dewey 338; Taft 203; Willkie 171

3rd: Dewey 315; Willkie 259; Taft 212

4th: Willkie 306; Taft 253; Dewey 250

5th: Willkie 429; Taft 377; Dewey 57

In the November election, Franklin Delano Roosevelt, as the Democratic nominee with his charm and inherent political strength, won a third term. Willkie made a good campaign, but no one could have defeated President Roosevelt that year, with World War II in full swing in Europe.

"Damn Fool"

✳✳✳✳

In my 36 years in elected public office, the most important political decision that ever I made was March 17, 1970.

It was on that date, via state-wide television, I told the Virginia people that I would seek re-election to the U. S. Senate as an Independent. (A full copy of the text of the speech is included following the end of this chapter.) Previously, I had been elected to public office seven times as a Democrat.

In February, the Democratic State Central Committee decreed that anyone seeking the Democratic nomination must sign an oath to support for president whoever the Democrats nominated two years hence.

I told the Virginia people that I could not, and would not, sign an oath two years before a candidate was chosen. And, I added, "I would rather be a free man than a captive senator."

Thus, since I could not enter the Democratic primary, I would take my record to the people of Virginia independent of either party.

There were for me anxious hours – and days – until I could get some indication as to the reaction of my colleagues in the Senate, but especially the reaction of the individual voters throughout the state.

Senator James O. Eastland of Mississippi and I were having lunch together, just the two of us. He had been in the Senate for 28 years and was fourth in seniority. We were close friends. He brought up the subject of my campaign and asked who would be my campaign manager.

I told him I hadn't fully decided, but was thinking of a newspaperman, the editor and general manager of one of my newspapers, a man with whom I had worked for 15 years.

Jim put down his knife and fork. He looked me squarely in the eyes and said, "You are a damn fool. First, you are going to run for re-election as an Independent, and that's a fool thing to do. And now you are going to have a damn newspaperman who doesn't know anything about politics as your campaign manager."

"That's right, Jim, but Lathan Mims and I have worked together for 15 years. He knows how I think. He can make decisions without talking with me. And, most importantly, I know if he is doubtful about a course of action, he will consult with me. He has solid judgment and I trust him completely."

As we finished lunch and were leaving the table, Jim, now friendly, said, "I have been thinking about what you plan to do – I figure you want to run your own campaign."

"You are 100 percent correct," I replied. "I know exactly how I want it run."

As it turned out, that "damn newspaperman" ran the best campaign of the many in which I have been involved.

From the press, I received this reaction. *TIME* magazine's appraisal: "Byrd is the end of a dynasty of true conservatives," said one knowledgeable Senate aide.

"His state is no longer conservative. Young Harry is out of step."

TIME added: "His chances are poor, and Byrd may well finish third in a three-way race."

To myself, I acknowledged that this probably was the statewide consensus.

On March 19, 1970, a *Norfolk Virginian Pilot* editorial said: "One may doubt the wisdom, but scarcely the sincerity, of Byrd's action." The Pilot said Byrd was "abandoning as near a sure victory as may be imagined in Virginia politics for a highly uncertain cause that invites double opposition."

Explaining Myself

✳✳✳✳

Following is the speech in which I revealed and explained my decision to the people of Virginia, March 17, 1970:

My dear fellow-Virginians,

I would like to think out loud with those whom I have the high honor - and the great responsibility - to represent in the Senate of the United States.

I love Virginia. I love every area of Virginia - every mountain, every valley, every seashore. And I love her people.

Our people are, I feel, forward - looking, responsible and moderate. We realize, too, that those of us representing the public must be attuned to the 1970s. We realize that times and conditions change - but that fundamental principles do not.

As you know, I have spent most of my adult life serving the people of Virginia to the best of my capabilities. For 18 years I served in the Senate of Virginia. I am now in my fifth year in the Senate of the United States.

During the past four sessions of the Congress, I have cast more than 1,000 recorded votes. My votes, my speeches, my views are a matter of record. This is available to all.

I cannot change that record. I would not change it if I could. I realize that no one will agree with every vote, but in each of them I have voted my convictions.

I have fought for the programs of the President - Democrat or Republican - when I thought he was right. I have fought against the programs of the President - Democrat or Republican - when I thought he was wrong.

I have acted independently of party lines. But I feel I have acted in the best interests of Virginia and of our nation. I have maintained that independence because I believe Virginians are independent, free-thinking people.

My term as United States Senator expires next January. This coming November, Virginians will vote to determine whom they wish to represent them in the United States Senate for the following six years.

I have given considerable thought as to how I can best submit my record to the voters of Virginia for their approval or disapproval.

The problems which face our nation are immense - both at home and abroad. The war. Inflation. Civil unrest. Crime. Pollution of air and water. Unrestrained government spending. Heavy taxation.

There is no Democratic solution to these problems; there is no Republican solution.

Party labels mean less and less to Virginians - and, indeed, to most Americans. They know that it is principle, rather than labels, upon which this nation was built.

In this modern age, more and more Virginians are thinking in terms of the general election. Fewer and fewer are participating in primaries. The best evidence of this was last year's gubernatorial primary. It drew fewer than one-fourth of the qualified voters.

Another important factor must be taken into consideration.

During 1969, the various candidates for Governor spent a total of $3 million. This is a staggering sum. Never before in Virginia have such huge sums been spent to achieve public office.

This is a deplorable trend. It discourages many from seeking public office. It could lead to undue influence.

Virginia, long noted for its integrity in high office, must not go the way of other states where elections are decided by wild spending.

Obviously, two election campaigns - a primary followed by a general election - would be twice as expensive as one campaign. Is this in the best interests of the people of Virginia?

I have listed two factors in my thinking.

Now we come to the most important.

Last month the Democratic State Central Committee took an unprecedented step. For the first time in 40 years, a Virginia Senator, if he is to seek re-election in the Democratic primary, will be required to sign an oath that he will support for President whoever is selected by the Democratic National Convention.

Veteran political writer John F. Daffron reported for The Associated Press the actions of the committee in these words:

> *"RICHMOND (AP) - The Virginia Democratic Party agreed yesterday to require candidates for office to pledge support of all Democratic nominees from the courthouse to the White House."*

The Committee is within its rights to require such an oath. I do not contest its action.

But this action has made it impossible for me to file in the Democratic primary.

I cannot, and will not, sign an oath to vote for and support an individual whose identity I do not know and whose principles and policies are thus unknown.

To sign such a blank check would be, I feel, the height of irresponsibility and unworthy of a member of the United States Senate.

I have given this matter a great deal of thought

since the committee action three weeks ago.

I am told that I could sign such an oath and forget it.

Perhaps there is a technicality behind which I could hide, but the intent of the committee requirement is clear.

Whatever I do, I want to do in good faith.

One reason Americans, and especially our young people, have become cynical about persons in public life is because too many politicians have become cynical, saying one thing prior to election and feeling free to do something else after election.

No one knows today who will be the Democratic nominee for President in 1972 - nor who will be the Republican nominee. No one knows what philosophy they will advocate.

The year 1972 will be a crucial one for our nation.

Before making a decision as to whom I shall support for President, I want to know the alternatives - and just where each candidate stands on the dominant issues.

To forfeit now my right to do this is to me unthinkable.

I had thought that this matter of a loyalty oath had been settled 18 years ago when Virginia's Governor John S. Battle told the 1952 Democratic National

Convention in these words . . . "We in Virginia are not going to sign any pledge or any commitment which will prevent freedom of thought and freedom of action."

Governor Battle made this statement in the convention four days before a presidential candidate was chosen. I would be required to subscribe to an oath two years before a candidate is chosen.

I am anxious to serve the people of Virginia in the United States Senate. I love our country, and I feel I can continue to make a contribution to Virginia and to the nation as a United States Senator.

Occasionally there comes a time when one must break with precedent, when one must do the unusual.

For me, such a time has come.

I shall take a fresh approach - to some, perhaps, a bold approach.

At this particular time - in this particular situation - in this particular election - I feel I can best serve Virginia by taking my record directly to all of the people in Virginia in November.

Now is not the time - it is too early - to announce my candidacy for the Senate. But being an independent Democrat I shall, at the appropriate time, file as an Independent in order to preserve my freedom of action.

I realize full well the difficulties I face in this decision. The course I am taking is an uncharted one.

But I would rather be a free man than a captive

senator.

I want and need the support of all Virginians -
Democrats, Republicans, Independents.

At a later date - between now and November - I
shall discuss in detail my Senate record, and I shall
continue to make known my views on the great issues
facing our nation.

I have been independent in casting my votes in
Washington, and I shall take only one oath - and that to
the people of Virginia: To conscientiously and impar-
tially serve all the people of our great state.

600 Holes Of Golf In 4 Days

❋❋❋❋

J. Smith Ferebee of Richmond was chairman of the finance committee for my 1970 campaign. He was a dynamic and remarkable individual, in whom one could have complete confidence.

A native Virginian, he attended the Virginia Military Institute, and then went to Chicago during the Depression to earn a living. Later, he became the top producer for the Equitable Life Assurance Society, the huge insurance company.

In 1970, he took early retirement from Equitable to raise funds for my campaign. A formidable task it was, especially so because I ran as an Independent and had no help from either political party.

That did not bother Smith. He liked challenges and had agreed to raise funds, before knowing whether I would run as a Democrat, Republican, or Independent.

What follows next dramatizes the kind of person Smith Ferebee was, and should be of interest to every golfer.

On the day after the bombing of Pearl Harbor, he volunteered for the Navy, fully intending to become a flyer. But the Navy said he was too old to fly.

Instead, Lieutenant Ferebee established and became the first executive officer of a naval flight instructor school at the Lewis School of Aeronautics in Lockport, Ill.

In true Ferebee fashion, he made the Lockport school the best of its type, and in his spare time learned to fly. At 37, having proved himself, he was awarded his wings – the oldest naval officer with no flight experience prior to military service to receive them. George H. W. Bush was the youngest.

Soon after, Smith was transferred to the carrier *Belleau Wood* in the Pacific. When he was shot down on a mercy mission over Japan, he became the last naval officer to be taken prisoner in that country.

After his release, with the rank of commander, he spent several months in the hospital recovering from serious injuries. Doctors who treated him said he would never play golf again. But they didn't know J. Smith Ferebee. To those who did, Ferebee's golf exploits were already legendary. At 31, he wagered $2,500 and half a Virginia estate that he could shoot 144 holes of golf between dawn and dusk. He did, and he didn't stop there. He next bet he could play 600 holes of golf in four days in eight different cities.

With a chartered DC-3, two pilots, a doctor, a nurse, and an official scorekeeper waiting, Ferebee teed off in Los Angeles on Sept. 25, 1938. During the four-day stint, he played 84 holes in Los Angeles, 81 in

Phoenix, 72 in Kansas City, 72 in St. Louis, 75 in Milwaukee, 72 in Chicago, 72 in Philadelphia, and 72 in New York, finishing with a putt at the World's Fair. He averaged slightly over 85 strokes per round, exhausted 110 caddies, walked or ran 180 miles, lost 21 pounds...and collected $25,000.

But golf was not his only sport. In 1949 he shot 2,400 rounds of skeet in four hours and 18 minutes, breaking 85 percent of the targets.

His exploits received nationwide publicity through articles in *Sports Illustrated, Ford Times, Life, The New Yorker* and other popular magazines. And he was named to the Virginia Sports Hall of Fame.

In early February of 1970, he called a meeting of 30 persons to ask them to join him on my fund-raising committee. We met at a motel near Richmond.

Opening the meeting, I said frankly I did not know just how I would run so I knew it was asking a lot for anyone to become a member of Smith's committee, thus giving me, in effect, a blank check not in financial, but political terms.

I spoke about 20 minutes, then left and returned to Washington so the group could have a full and frank discussion without being encumbered by my presence.

Smith told me later that 26 of the 30 signed on. Four wanted to wait until I determined how I would run. Three of the four came aboard later.

Smith said, "Harry, your job is to attend to your Senate responsibilities: voting, office work, committee work, campaigning.

"We will do the fund-raising. We will not interfere with you, and we prefer you not interfere with us." That was music to my ears.

But, I did greatly disappoint Smith on at least one occasion.

An enthusiastic Smith phoned me at my Senate office to say the mail brought two large checks – $5,000 each – the largest he had received. (We had put a limit of $5,000 from any one person or group).

When he told me the names of the mother and daughter mailing the contributions, I told Smith I was sorry, but I must ask him to return both contributions. My problem was that I had taken an active interest in legislation they favored.

In actual fact, neither mother nor daughter would gain personally from the legislation which was enacted. The daughter was a trustee of a tax-exempt charitable foundation and she wanted a law to require tax-exempt organizations to pay a higher percentage of the funds to charity. It was a worthy cause and national in scope.

I asked Ferebee to return the contributions to forestall charges by political opponents that I received campaign funds from persons I helped with legislation, although it was for a good cause and easily explained.

But a candidate can be damaged by being forced to explain something he has done.

My Favorite Editorial

✳✳✳✳

During my campaign for re-election to the U. S. Senate as an Independent, my favorite editorial was the reaction of *The Washington Post* to my announcement that I would seek re-election as an Independent, although I had been elected to public office seven times as a Democrat.

There is no doubt that the state was taken by surprise. The early reaction was muted, but it heated quickly. On Wednesday, my office was bombarded by the news media. I kept out of sight and refused all requests for interviews. I remember Jack Davis, who almost always kept his cool, got quite annoyed with me for refusing a press conference.

I told him to tell the news media that I would have a full-scale press conference at the John Marshall Hotel in Richmond at 2 p.m. that Thursday, but not before.

Jack was not happy that I put it off that long – four news cycles after the original announcement. But I wanted my reasons to sink in before new quotes from me could be obtained.

I loved that news conference. My statement to the Virginia people had not attacked anyone. In fact, I had asserted that the Democratic Central Committee was within its rights to require a loyalty pledge – I did not ask that the pledge be rescinded.

Since it was difficult to attack my speech, the focus was kept where I wanted it: The committee had the right to require the pledge – and I had the right to refuse.

At the press conference Thursday, I answered questions for 35 minutes.

Among the questions: Did I plan to start a third political party?

Answer: "No. The decision I was forced to make is a personal one; it involved no one else.

"It is a decision for this particular time, this particular election, this particular situation.

"Whether it's the politically wise decision can only be determined in November, but I believe it's the right decision.

"I hope my Senate record will have the support of a majority of Democrats, a majority of Republicans, a majority of Independents."

Question: Would your father have signed the loyalty oath?

Answer: "No, I don't think so. But the difference is this: He would have made the decision in 24 hours. It took me three weeks."

But, what made the news conference so much fun for me – and which, I thought, made several important points for my benefit – was *The Washington Post* editorial the morning after my announcement. *The Post* castigated me for my course of action.

I took *The Post* editorial with me and held it up and read the two key points, namely, Byrd's action made it impossible for Virginia's fine new Republican governor – the first Republican governor in the 20th century – to elect a Republican senator.

I read it slowly, wanting to focus on it a bit. I did not criticize *The Post*. Indeed, I said, perhaps The Post was right. What I didn't say, but what was in my mind, was that the more this assertion was accepted by Democrats, the more it would ease the shock of my leaving the Democratic Party.

In the short run it would hurt me with Republicans, but before the campaign was over, I felt I could make it a plus. I had confidence that if a Republican couldn't be elected, as The Post asserted, most Republicans would prefer me to a Democrat.

The second point *The Post* made was even more beneficial to me. The editorial said I didn't have to run as an Independent. Rather, the editorial said the pledge "seems to us to be more of an excuse."

The Post said Byrd could run as a Democrat simply by signing the oath required by the Democratic committee, and then, after the election, ignore the pledge. *The Post* added that that's what most Southern

Democratic senators would do.

Here again, I did not criticize *The Post*. I said The Post had a point, and its suggestion did cross my mind. But, I asked myself, was that the kind of senator the Virginia people wanted?

I repeated, yes, I could have done what *The Post* recommended. But if I had done that, would I have been worthy of representing the people of Virginia in the U. S. Senate?

I found *The Washington Post* editorial to be a valuable campaign tool. I carried it with me for weeks.

Attitude Of
The Nixon White House

✳✳✳✳

Richard Nixon and I had been friends since he was elected to the Senate in 1950. We saw quite a bit of each other when he became vice president, two years later.

In 1969, soon after he became president, he invited me to the Oval Office and authorized me to contact him personally if there should be anything I wanted from his administration.

I gave him strong support in his efforts to end the Vietnam War. He talked with me about six or seven names he was considering for Supreme Court appointments.

We were friends who, despite different party affiliation, felt we could talk in confidence to each other. Whatever commitments he made to me, he kept. (That is more than I can say for some other presidents.)

With 1970 being the year of my re-election run, the President talked with me several times about becoming a Republican. I listened but gave no indication of doing so. Key White House staff took a harder line in pressuring me.

As the date of the Republican state convention

got nearer, I received a phone call from Bryce Harlow, a fine, able Nixon aide. I had worked with him on legislation from time to time.

Bryce phoned me one Friday morning in May or June and asked me to join him for lunch at The White House. I sensed what he wanted to discuss and told him I had a luncheon commitment. He then asked if he could meet with me in my office. We set the time at 3 p.m.

After I became an Independent, I likened myself, in my own mind, to the man on his death bed to whom the priest was giving the last rites. When the priest asked, "Do you denounce the devil and all his works," the sick one replied, "In my condition, I don't denounce anyone."

Running against both political parties, I didn't want to make anyone mad unnecessarily.

So I listened to Bryce, and said very little.

A real gentleman, he calmly outlined the many disadvantages facing an Independent, and then cited the advantages of becoming the Republican nominee.

Here again I said little but did point out that I had been elected to public office seven times as a Democrat, had been treated very well by the Democratic Senate, had the best committee assignments – and all of this despite the fact I voted frequently with Republicans on legislation.

President Richard M. Nixon tried unsuccessfully to get Senator Byrd to run as a Republican in the 1970 U.S. Senate election in Virginia. The two are pictured together above in a photo from the 1950s when Nixon was Vice President.

Bryce changed tactics a bit and then got to what he probably thought was his major point, his heaviest artillery.

"Senator," he said, "you probably want to know how we can guarantee you the Republican Senate nomination. The White House staff has thought a great deal about this and we have worked out a plan to assure a successful result.

"Here is what we will do. The President will have Governor Holton come to The White House, and the President and the governor – the national leader and the state leader – will put their arms around you and say, 'Harry's our man.' That will assure you the nomination."

Indeed it would, no doubt about that.

But I felt it also could severely damage my credibility and put me under obligation to Nixon, to Holton, and to the Republican Party. It also would be inconsistent with what I told the Virginia people on March 17.

I kept my cool; I didn't comment on the proposal, but thanked him for coming to see me. We had been talking 2 1/2 hours.

Bryce, sensing that I was not enchanted with the plan he presented, tried one more pitch: "Senator, the White House staff has given this Virginia election a tremendous amount of thought. The White House staff says you cannot win as an Independent."

At that point, I lost my cool.

I said, "Bryce," – and I remember these words well – "You tell the White House staff that I am willing to concede that the White House staff may know more than I do about every conceivable subject, except two, Virginia and Virginia politics. You tell the White House staff that I am going to run as an Independent, and I am going to be elected as an Independent."

Bryce kept <u>his</u> cool, and said, "Senator, I can see you really mean it."

Beginning Of 1970 Campaign

****

I began my campaign for re-election to the U. S. Senate on the night of Thursday, Sept. 10.

That "Byrd for Senate" 8 p.m. rally was held in Chesterfield County at Manchester High School.

The weather was not cooperative. It rained most of the day, and heavily between 6 and 7 p.m. I could see headlines the next day – "Small Crowd Attends Independent's Rally, Suggests Byrd in Trouble."

In my mind's eye, I could see the pounding I would get from the news media: "Few Attend Independent's Campaign Rally."

At 7:30 the rain had lightened, but still drizzling; the school grounds were soaked. But cars were everywhere.

I began to feel better. The reception committee taking me from the car to a side door of the school seemed, I thought, more enthusiastic than warranted.

But when Kenneth Timmons, my campaign manager for Chesterfield County and the chairman of the night's rally, escorted me to the stage to a standing-room-only crowd, it was a sight that is still in my mind 36 years later. And when Ken whispered to me that there were several hundred more outside the hall for whom loudspeakers had been set up, it added frosting to the attendance cake.

Seated on the platform during the preliminaries, and observing the packed crowd – as well as the multitude of TV cameras and the horde of reporters – I lost my foreboding about the rain.

I became geared up, fired up.

The television cameras ground away, the crowd was so enthusiastic that I bore down hard on each of the various points that I wanted to get across. The frequent applause caused me to forget how hot the auditorium was that September night, the heat enhanced by the television lights.

The news accounts the next day said I spoke 32 minutes and was interrupted by applause 40 times.

When the speech was over, and after an hour of hand-shaking with those in the audience, my shirt, my suit, and my body were as wet as if I had been submerged in a swimming pool.

For me, it was a night to be remembered – even to this day.

What a wonderful way to start a campaign.

The reception I received from the people of Chesterfield County was so heartwarming, I resolved that any subsequent campaigns of mine would kick off at the same place, same time, same date.

For this campaign, the 9th Congressional District

was by far the most difficult for me. The 9th is in the mountainous southwestern part of our state, beginning south of Roanoke and running to the Tennessee and Kentucky lines. It is home to the state's coal mines, the major coal-mining counties being Wise, Tazewell, Russell, Buchanan, and Dickenson.

Historically, in the 9th, there is no such thing as an Independent. The voters there are either Republican or Democrat. There is no middle ground. The 9th takes its politics very seriously, much more so than any of the now 11 congressional districts in Virginia.

From the date I announced as an Independent, I felt I could survive if I did not lose the 9th by more than 20,000 to 25,000 votes.

In making numerous phone calls to key political friends in the 9th, I soon found that not many desired "the pleasure of my company." Many said they were for me and wanted me elected and would help me quietly, but thought it better to keep my campaigning there to a minimum. I fully understood.

I needed to show activity, however, and made some unnecessary and unproductive trips merely for the purpose of physically being in the 9th District.

I had support in both political parties, but for the most part the vocal efforts on my behalf were from individual citizens, rather than from political leaders.

My basic strategy for the 9th was to get there

from time to time with no particular purpose in mind, and to try to get some radio and newspaper coverage to show I was not neglecting that beautiful part of our state.

I don't recall that we ever had a district-wide rally. As Election Day approached, I feared for the worst.

I was delighted when the votes were counted on Nov. 3 and I had polled 30.7 percent of the total vote cast, against George Rawlings' 37.6 percent and Roy Garland's 31.6 percent.

Thus I lost the 9th by approximately 6,000 votes – so much better than the heavy loss I had expected. I ran third in a three-way race there, but a close third.

Both Political Parties
Sought My Defeat

****

Between the three-month period after my announcement as an Independent in 1970 and the state Republican convention on June 26, Republicans debated hotly as to whether the convention should or should not nominate a candidate against me.

Sentiment within the Republican Party was divided. I had developed through the years many friends and supporters within the party. My voting record was generally acceptable to the average Republican.

GOP leaders, too, were split over whether to endorse my Independent candidacy for re-election or to nominate a Republican to run against me.

The chairman of the Republican National Committee, Rogers C. B. Morton, said, "Byrd's Independent run suggests an excellent opportunity for an outstanding Republican to capture Byrd's seat."

Virginia Governor A. Linwood Holton continued the leadership role in the effort to put forward a GOP contender. Years later, he offered this explanation to Frank Atkinson, author of *"The Dynamic Dominion"*: "This has been my life – to build a two-party system in Virginia. And one year after we had first elected a statewide candidate was not the time to throw up our hands and concede the election to an Independent."

Atkinson's book quoted Holton as saying, "I like Harry Byrd personally, but his thinking and my thinking are different, particularly on this race issue (the busing of school children to achieve racial balance, a dominant issue in 1970)."

In a decisive banquet speech the night before the convention session, Holton urged delegates to field a candidate, saying: "I have seen speculation in the papers that you will go home having done nothing. Frankly, I can't believe it. We are the biggest, strongest, and the best party in Virginia... I can't believe we will do nothing. Doing nothing would be like having the biggest, shiniest fire engine and not taking it to the fire."

Republican Congressman Joel Broyhill, who at that point had represented Northern Virginia in the U. S. House of Representatives for 18 years and was seeking re-election, was outspoken for me. He was leading the fight against the governor's position, and urged that no nomination be made. The Nixon White House sent a representative to back up Broyhill.

Congressman Broyhill, able and courageous, made a valiant effort on my behalf, taking on the full strength of the newly elected Republican governor. But in his zeal to help me, he made a statement on the eve of the convention that presented a problem for me. He said he "knew I would vote with the Republicans to organize the Senate, if the Republican state convention did not give him opposition."

I was in my office in Washington when my campaign manager, Lathan Mims, telephoned me from Richmond with Broyhill's words.

I knew I had to act immediately – and I did so within minutes. Silence at this point, would, I thought, mislead the convention, and damage my Independent stance. I told the press that Joel was expressing only what he thought I would do. I said, "I have made no commitments to anyone, except public commitments to all the people of Virginia." I regretted my necessity to damage Joel's efforts on my behalf. I said I would welcome a convention endorsement, but could make no promises in order to get it.

When the roll was called, the governor's position prevailed by the vote of 644 - 420.

I regarded this as a victory for me, and for the Broyhill forces, because I had obtained the votes of 40 percent of the Republican activists. To me, this meant that I would get a high percentage of the rank-and-file Republican voters in November.

The Republican nominee chosen by the convention was Ray Garland, a two-term member of the House of Delegates.

Garland's nomination was a major triumph for Governor Holton, whose leadership had been decisive in defeating the pro-Byrd effort.

The U. S. Senate that year did not adjourn until Oct. 14. Thus, I had only two weeks for full-time campaigning.

Throughout my Senate career I always had taken the position that when the Senate was in session, my primary responsibility was to be there to vote. I had a 97 percent voting participation record, and even though the campaign was on, I felt an obligation to be at the Senate.

Both of my opponents kept demanding a debate. I replied that "I don't have time to educate Mr. (George) Rawlings and Mr. Garland, but that I would get them seats in the Senate gallery and they could hear my speeches from there."

My campaign emphasized, too, that my record was well-known and that neither of them had a record that could justify debate.

After the Senate adjourned Oct. 14, I was full-time on the campaign trail.

And I began my campaign dietary regimen – a 12-ounce sirloin steak for breakfast. That way I could get by with little to eat – a glass of milk for lunch, and a light dinner. (I don't eat much if I have a speech to make, as was always the case at night).

My Democratic opponent called me the Republican from Winchester, as in the Senate I voted a great deal with the Republicans on legislative matters. My Republican opponent said I was too much of a Democrat, as I voted with the Democrats on procedural matters. I said both opponents were right.

Rawlings called Byrd "a do-nothing, vote-no, so-called senator." Garland attacked Byrd as "system-wrecker."

The Washington Post reported "a stinging attack" on Byrd by Holton and Garland campaigning together.

The Post reported that the two Republicans said Byrd would bring a multi-party system to Virginia; Holton told audiences "an Independent candidate has about as much place in the Senate as a kangaroo."

In my speeches I emphasized that I was running on my Senate record, saying, "I could not change my record if I would; I would not change it if I could."

Throughout 1970, I kept two maxims in mind: one, don't shoot until you see the whites of your opponent's eyes; and, two, once a decision is made, "damn the torpedoes, full steam ahead."

On Oct. 20, Rogers C. B. Morton, the national chairman of the Republican Party, came to Virginia to seek support for Mr. Garland. Earlier, on Oct. 17, the Garland camp brought to Richmond Senator Robert Packwood of Oregon. Senator Packwood, in his speeches in Virginia, said "we need a young leader like Mr. Garland. He's my kind of man."

In my speeches I quoted the senator from Oregon and said that one is justified in assuming that if elected my Republican opponent would vote similarly to Mr. Packwood.

Then I said, "Let's look at Mr. Packwood's voting record."

• The Oregon senator was part of a hard-core group in the Senate determined to block any Southerner nominated to the Supreme Court.

• He voted against President Nixon's Supreme Court nominees, both Southerners.

• He voted against legislation for freedom of choice as to which school to attend.

• He voted in favor of forced busing of school children to achieve racial balance, taking them many miles from their homes and from their neighborhood schools.

• Despite President Nixon's plea, the Oregon senator voted against a bill aimed at controlling crime in the District of Columbia.

After citing these votes, and emphasizing that Senator Packwood said my Republican opponent was "his kind of man," I emphasized that "I am not Packwood's kind of man," and that I voted against the way Packwood voted on all these important issues.

So, I said, according to Senator Packwood, the Virginia people have a clear-cut choice: They can vote for "his kind of man" or they can vote for me.

The best I could judge the Packwood foray into Virginia was not especially successful, as Mr. Garland spent the next week denying he would vote the same way as Mr. Packwood.

Having one's opponent on the defensive is my idea of a good campaign.

Election Day 1970

✳✳✳✳

As every reader can well imagine, the night of November 3, 1970 was, for me, the night of a lifetime. First returns from the voting began to come in about 8 p.m. The results were favorable right from the beginning – but continually got better. When it appeared I might get a majority of the vote – more than the combined total of my two opponents – I found it difficult to believe.

My first thoughts were those of deep appreciation to the people of Virginia. The people had given me a "blank check," authorizing me to vote as I felt was best for the nation without regard to political party. Never before in the history of the United States Senate had anyone received more votes than the nominees of both the major parties combined, and only once before (George Norris of Nebraska, 1936) had anyone been elected against opposition from both major parties.

Former Governor Mills Godwin made the following statement:

"This has been a truly great day for Virginia. Senator Byrd has scored a landslide victory. It emphasizes again the philosophy which made this nation great and which Virginia clearly desires to preserve."

Here are the final results:

Byrd (Ind.)	506,237	54%
Garland (Rep.)	147,765	15%
Rawlings (Dem.)	294,582	31%

Byrd carried 121 of the 134 counties and cities in Virginia.

Rawlings carried 10.

Garland carried only Dickinson, Scott and Carroll, all in the southwest part of the state.

In Norfolk, the state's most populous city, Rawlings won by less than 500 votes:

Rawlings	20,867
Byrd	20,371
Garland	4,683

Rawlings carried only three cities, Galax and Norton in the Southwest and Norfolk.

Garland lost every city, including his home city of Roanoke.

Byrd carried nine of the 10 congressional districts, losing only the 9th where he ran behind both Rawlings and Garland.

General Election for U.S. Senate, 1970 by Counties

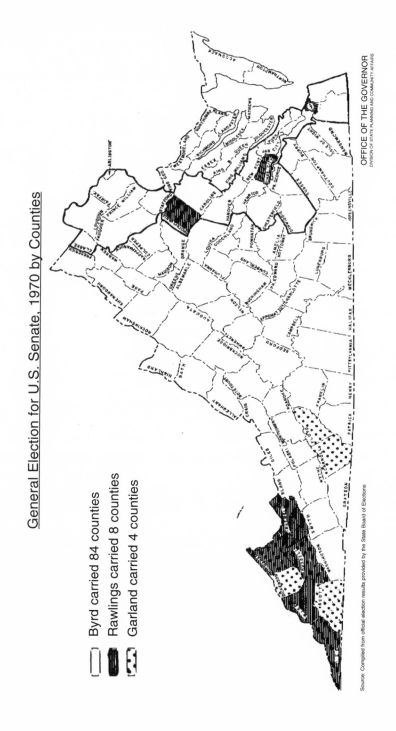

Byrd carried 84 counties

Rawlings carried 8 counties

Garland carried 4 counties

OFFICE OF THE GOVERNOR
DIVISION OF STATE PLANNING AND COMMUNITY AFFAIRS

General Election for U.S. Senate, 1970 by Cities

Byrd carried 36 cities

Rawlings carried 3 cities

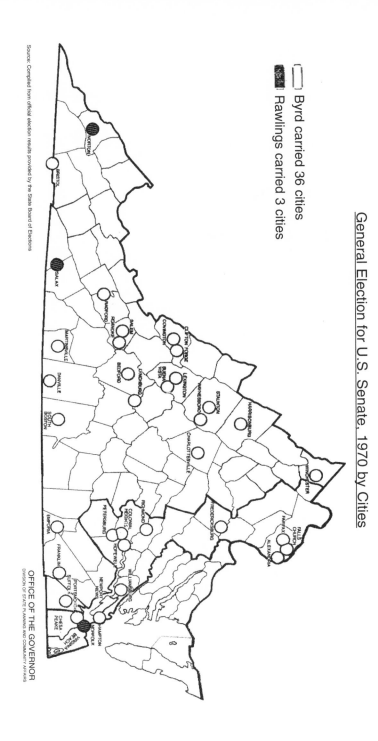

Source: Compiled from official election results provided by the State Board of Elections

OFFICE OF THE GOVERNOR
DIVISION OF STATE PLANNING AND COMMUNITY AFFAIRS

TIME reported:
"Byrd is the end of a dynasty of true conservatives," said one knowledgeable Senate aide. "His state is no longer conservative. Young Harry is out of step."

TIME added:
. . . his chances are poor, and Byrd may well finish third in a three-way race.
—March 30, 1970

TOMORROW
SNOW: RAIN

Winchester Evening Star

75th Year No. 104

WINCHESTER, VIRGINIA 22601, WEDNESDAY, NOVEMBER 4, 1970

2 SECTIONS-2
32-PAGES-32

Byrd Wins In Landslide Victory;
His Total Exceeds Half-Million

Senator Gets 75 Per Cent Of Area Vote

Rawlings, Garland Trail in Big Turnout

Automatic Tax Reduction

✳✳✳✳

In 1946, at the beginning of Virginia Governor William Tuck's administration, the General Assembly increased income taxes. By 1950 (I was elected to the state Senate in 1948), there was a public outcry that caused me to take a look at the issue – not to repeal the increase but, perhaps, to modify it.

With a lot of help, I developed a piece of legislation which I titled "AUTOMATIC TAX REDUCTION."

In brief, it said: The legislature may appropriate whatever amount of money it feels necessary to meet Virginia's needs, but if tax revenues exceed the amount considered necessary, then income taxes the following year would be reduced by a similar percentage.

That proposal was in effect for four years during which time there were annual income tax reductions of between 12 percent and 16 percent.

In 1953 the Maryland State Senate invited me to appear before its Finance Committee to explain my Virginia plan. Some in the Maryland Legislature wanted to consider it for Maryland taxpayers. I accepted Maryland's invitation.

This led to one of the most dismal, but also one of

55

the most exhilarating, experiences I've had.

I arrived late one Monday afternoon to address the legislative committee on Tuesday morning. To my surprise, the Senate asked me to address its 29 members at its Monday night session. Since I had no advance notice, I had nothing prepared.

The Senate doors were locked, no visitors allowed, and I was called upon for a speech. I don't remember what I discussed, but when I concluded, the response was dismal, hardly a ripple. I felt worse than I can ever remember. It was only after I left the Senate chamber that I learned there was a sharply divided Senate, voting 14-14 on almost every subject.

The next day I was asked to attend a session of the House of Delegates. After the flop I had made the previous evening, I said I would prefer not to accept the House invitation. I finally agreed on condition the presiding officer would not call on me for a speech.

The presiding officer gave me a fine introduction, then said, "The Senator from Virginia is most welcome and this legislative body would appreciate a speech of his own choosing."

My worse fears had been realized.

I spoke for 8-10 minutes and have no recollection as to what I said. But when I concluded, the entire legislative body gave me a standing ovation with prolonged applause.

Remembering the flop I made the night before, the very favorable reaction from the House was one of the most gratifying I ever had.

Harold Vanderbilt

✳✳✳✳

In 1952, Harold Stirling Vanderbilt, (1884-1970) of the famous and wealthy Vanderbilt family, had a summer home in Shenandoah County, one of the counties I then represented in the Virginia Senate.

Harold was associated with the New York Central Railroad and was also notable as the inventor of the game of contract bridge and as the skilled yachtsman who won the America's Cup three times.

He sent word that he would like to meet me and asked that I visit him. This I did.

Mr. Vanderbilt explained that he was interested in helping one of the statewide political candidates and handed me two $5,000 checks. He said he thought I would know better how to use them effectively than would he.

The election came with his candidate being successful.

The next time I went through Shenandoah County I stopped by his home, meeting him in his living room. After explaining some of the aspects of the campaign, I told him that I did not need both checks and thus wanted to return one of them. He seemed startled, but did not say a word.

He left the room, went to the steps and called for his wife to come to meet him in the living room.

In my mind, and waiting for them, I could not figure what was wrong and thought surely he would not be mad with me for returning one of the checks. I just sat by myself and waited. When the two returned to the living room, Harold showed the check to his wife and said, "I want you to see this check. This is the first time in more than a hundred years that anyone has ever given a Vanderbilt anything."

A month later, he asked me to join his wife and him as the third trustee of a multi-million-dollar trust fund for the benefit of Shenandoah County Hospital.

Governor Tuck

✻✻✻✻

William M. Tuck, from Halifax County, was elected to the Virginia House of Delegates, state Senate, lieutenant governor, and governor (1946-50). Later he became a member of the U.S. House of Representatives for the 5th Congressional District.

He was a delightful person, a close friend, and a confidant.

In February 1958, he phoned me that he wanted to drive to Winchester the next day to discuss an important matter. The next day a heavy snowstorm hit Virginia. The trip being a long one, he arrived at my home about 6 p.m.

Prior to his arrival, I had a phone call from a local subscriber to The Winchester Star, of which I was publisher, saying he had not yet received that day's afternoon paper. I agreed he was entitled to it and I would phone the office to have it delivered.

The former governor and I had just begun our discussion and were preparing to have dinner when the phone rang again. It was the same individual, saying he still had not received that day's Star. I said, "I will bring it to you."

When I left the phone, I asked Governor Tuck if I

could borrow his chauffeur-driven automobile, which had chains to maneuver in the snow.

Bill reluctantly agreed. His car and I reached the proper house on the north side of Winchester, where I delivered the paper. The customer insisted I come inside his home; that delayed me a bit.

When I returned, Bill said, "I come all the way across the state in a snowstorm to discuss some important matters with you and you leave just as we are starting to talk. You leave to deliver a newspaper. I have never known such a thing.

"But, if you ever run for the Senate, I would never run against someone who would take the time and trouble to deliver a newspaper in a snowstorm."

Vietnam

—————————— ✳✳✳✳ ——————————

When John F. Kennedy took office as President of the United States in 1961, he named Robert McNamara as Secretary of Defense.

Lyndon Johnson, succeeding the assassinated president, kept the Kennedy Cabinet, depending heavily on Secretary McNamara. The two greatly expanded the Vietnam war and, by 1966, had more than 500,000 troops in that country.

In 1967, I made a fact-finding trip to Vietnam for the Senate Armed Service Committee. Upon arrival, I was met by commanding General William Westmoreland's chief of staff. He told me a schedule had been arranged for me to gather information about the war. I told him I appreciated his help, but that I preferred to map my own schedule.

That night General Westmoreland, holding a dinner for me with his top military officers, said he understood these intentions. He told me he was turning over to me his executive jet with the authority to tell the pilots when and where to go.

I went to each of the five military areas beginning with the one nearest the DMZ, where the Marines were located. The commanding general there had a working luncheon for me with his senior officers, after which I went into the field, meeting individual junior officers, sergeants, corporals, and privates.

I repeated the same process at each of the other four military areas.

Everywhere I went, and almost everyone with whom I talked, gave me an entirely different "take" on conditions there, and what needed to be done, than we were getting in Washington from President Johnson and Secretary McNamara.

One of the Sundays I spent in the battle area, I accompanied the corps commander to a church service held in the open next to a field hospital. Following the service, we visited the hospital to talk with the wounded.

I must admit I was a bit distracted because my son, Tom, a Marine sergeant, was due for duty in Vietnam shortly. So in going through the hospital, I tended to associate him with the wounded.

When I returned to Washington, I made my report to the Senate Armed Services Committee and to the president.

Foremost in my report was the vital need to shut off supplies to the enemy coming through the Haiphong harbor. McNamara strongly opposed this proposal, which was being urged by his top generals in the field.

When the President nominated Townsend Hoopes

to be Under Secretary of the Air Force, I held up his confirmation when his name came before the Senate. After about 10 days, Secretary McNamara telephoned me to say it was most important to him that Mr. Hoopes be confirmed. McNamara asked to meet with me so he could impress on me what an important individual Hoopes was.

I said, "Bob, I have no problem with Mr. Hoopes. The problem is you. What I am doing is to dramatize my opposition to the way you and the President are running the war."

I did relent and Hoopes was confirmed. But I think my action helped a bit to focus attention on some unwise aspects of the handling of the war.

Over a period of time, I talked one-on-one with President Johnson four different times, stressing various aspects of my report, which reflected the views of the soldiers in the field. In each meeting he said that what we were doing was the way McNamara thought it should be handled. Thirty years later, McNamara wrote a book stating he knew in the 1960s the United States could not win the Vietnam war.

When I first went to the Senate in 1965, the Armed Services Committee was greatly impressed with, and had confidence in, Bob McNamara. By late 1967, two-thirds of that committee had totally lost confidence in him; Johnson finally kicked him upstairs, naming him president of The World Bank in 1968.

Incidentally, the first thing President Nixon did with regard to Vietnam when he assumed the presidency was to close the Haiphong harbor, thus shutting off the heavy supplies being delivered to the enemy.

Needed: Balanced Budget

***

During the 18 years I served in the U. S. Senate, I made a major effort to obtain an amendment to the constitution mandating that the Congress balance the federal budget. Deficits had been the rule, continually increasing the federal debt.

My observation had been that most members of the Congress have little interest in the subject. Indeed, too many individual citizens feel that if one gets something from the federal government, it doesn't cost anything.

Deficit spending has become a way of life. The accumulated annual deficits have now brought the total debt to $8 trillion, with huge interest payments to bondholders being added to the debt each year.

Over the years I have often thought that democratic government holds the seeds of its own destruction. I say that because it is obvious to me that the people's representatives in the Congress lack responsibility and abhor restraint, when it comes to spending public funds.

Only by an amendment to the constitution can spending be brought under control. When it comes to spending there is not much difference between the two political parties.

Through the years, hundreds of times, Jefferson's warning came to my thoughts:

"In questions of power, let no more be heard of confidence in man, but bind him down from mischief by the chains of the Constitution."

In 1978, I got enough votes in the Senate to require an amendment to the constitution. The Byrd amendment stated:

"SEC. 7 Beginning with fiscal year 1981, the total budget outlays of the Federal Government shall not exceed its receipts." Only 17 words.

Section 7 of Public Law 95-435 was approved by the Senate, approved by the House of Representatives, and signed into law by the President of the United States on Oct. 10, 1978.

What happened?

The Congress refused to obey its own law.

Home For The Vice President

✳✳✳✳

In 1973, following the resignation of Vice President Spiro Agnew, President Nixon chose Gerald Ford of Michigan, the Republican leader in the House of Representatives, to become vice president.

A few months later Vice President Ford asked me to meet with him in his ceremonial office just off the Senate chamber. He had with him his counselor, and my dear friend, John O. Marsh Jr.

Jerry told me that he and his wife, Betty, found it almost impossible to live in their small Alexandria home. The added Secret Service personnel, additional security equipment, and increase in house traffic, made life unbearable.

He asked if I would sponsor legislation to obtain a permanent residence for vice presidents.

I asked if he had a suggestion. He did – the home at the Naval Observatory on Massachusetts Avenue historically assigned to the Chief of Naval Operations, the occupant then being Admiral Elmo Zumwalt.

I questioned whether it would be large enough to house a family and also spacious enough to host conferences, entertain foreign officials, and other requirements expected of a vice president. He assured me it was.

To approve and fund a vice presidential residence would require congressional approval. I agreed to handle it, but first wanted to go through the house to see for myself whether it was adequate for future needs as a permanent home for a vice president.

My office made the necessary arrangements with Mrs. Zumwalt for a visit to the residence. She received me graciously, but it was obvious she was not at all happy (my action played a part in the subsequently retired Admiral Zumwalt's decision to run against me in my re-election campaign of 1976).

As a Naval officer during World War II, I was ambivalent about getting congressional approval to take this home away from the Chief of Naval Operations. But I thought a permanent home for the nation's vice president was important, and over the years would likely be more economical than remodeling individual homes as different individuals assume the second highest office in the land.

After the remodeling was completed, new furnishings were needed. That brought a phone call for another meeting with Gerald Ford. It was a short meeting.

The Vice President said his wife had a figure as to the cost of refurbishing. I asked him the cost. He said, "You wouldn't want to know, but I want you to tell me now that you will not approve Betty's figure."

Senator Byrd and President Gerald Ford were friends and colleagues for many years before Ford was appointed Vice President and later ascended to the presidency in 1974.

I asked him if I could know the figure. He said, "No, I just want you to tell me you won't approve it."

I said, "I won't approve it."

He turned to Jack Marsh and asked him to tell Betty that Senator Byrd refused to approve her figure.

I got a big kick out of that. Among other things, it proved how genuine Jerry Ford is. Like most husbands, he wanted somebody else to give the bad news to his wife.

Bahrain –
"I'm Out Of Here"

✴✴✴✴

In 1978, as a member of the Armed Services Committee, I went to the Middle East, to Saudi Arabia, Oman, and Egypt.

After a few days in Saudi Arabia, I met with King Khalid. After preliminary remarks he asked how I liked Saudi Arabia. I surmised he had a good sense of humor, so I replied by telling him I liked it fine except the government confiscated my whiskey. (My wife had put a pint of Scotch and a pint of vodka in my luggage.)

He laughed and said, "Well, you have to obey our laws."

In Bahrain, which is a very small country, there were two U. S. warships in the harbor. The captain of each asked that I board to shake hands with the crew. Which I did.

From the ships, I immediately went to the palace for a meeting with the emir. He started the conversation by saying, "You know we do not permit warships in our harbors."

I had just left two warships and had been aboard both, and shook hands with the crews. The emir knew they were there, and he knew that I knew they were only a couple of miles from his palace. His comments made clear to me that in the Middle East reality frequently takes a back seat to rhetoric.

During our conversation, his son, the foreign minister, was present. He would interrupt with hostile comments about the United States. I ignored the first two, but when the third interruption occurred, I said to the emir, "I am here as your guest. I appreciate your hospitality. But if that guy (and that's what I called him) makes one more hostile comment about my country, I'm out of here."

The emir didn't say a word, just lifted his right arm, made a gesture toward his son and that was the last we heard from the foreign minister.

In Oman, I did not see the king, but the foreign minister impressed me greatly and we had a fine visit. I learned a good bit from him.

I had planned to go from that country to Yemen, but the foreign minister in Oman told me that Yemen was a hostile country and dangerous. He said his secret service had brought him news that day that an insurrection in Yemen was imminent.

That got me to thinking as to whether to cancel plans for Yemen. I decided to do so because I had responsibility for a U.S. military plane with two American pilots and a Marine major as my military aide. It was my responsibility whether we canceled or not. I decided to cancel.

In Egypt, I was the guest of the Egyptian legislature. Three Egyptian senators had been assigned to escort me wherever I went. They were most gracious and most attentive. They even posted a guard at my hotel room.

On my final morning I had an early flight and, when I arrived in the hotel lobby with my Marine major escort, to my astonishment, the three Egyptian senators were waiting to take me to the airport. I gave my military aide the currency to pay for the hotel rooms.

It immediately brought excitement and almost anger. One senator kept saying that I was the guest of the Egyptian government and that they would regard it as an insult.

I replied that it was not intended as an insult. I said I appreciated their hospitality, but I wanted to pay my own way.

I was determined I would not be under any financial obligation to a foreign government.

Reducing The Estate Tax

✳✳✳✳

I am including this vignette for two reasons: first, it substantially benefitted taxpayers, and, second, it gives an indication of how laws are made, and the role sheer luck often plays.

In 1981, when President Reagan presented legislation to reduce income tax rates in stages from 70 percent to 50 percent, it did not include any change in the estate (death) tax.

Here's where the drama begins.

The Ways & Means Committee of the House of Representatives was chaired by Congressman Dan Rostenkowski of Chicago, who was strongly opposed to the Reagan legislation, as were most Democrats. So Rostenkowski, in an effort to defeat the Reagan plan, presented his own proposal. In seeking to obtain more votes to defeat the Reagan plan, Rostenkowski included a reduction in the estate tax.

The House passed his proposal, and later the Senate approved the president's bill. This caused a Committee of Conference to negotiate differences between the two bills.

The small conference committee, with representatives from each of the two houses, met with Mr.

Rostenkowski as chairman of the joint committee. On the Senate side, the chief negotiator for the president's position was Russell Long of Louisiana, chairman of the Finance Committee. I, as next in seniority, was also on the committee, along with Democratic Senator Lloyd Bentsen of Texas and Republican Senator Bob Dole of Kansas.

There were 400 different items in contention – many small, others quite important.

Rostenkowski went down the list one by one. When he reached Item 52, dealing with capital gains taxes, he read it, and immediately moved that the House position prevail. Three or four members of the joint committee protested that no discussion had been held and it could not be voted upon until the item had been debated.

Rostenkowski ruled everyone out of order and took a roll-call vote. The conferees on the House side voted unanimously with him.

At that point, I kept my attention focused on Item 117, the reduction in the estate tax which Rostenkowski himself had put in the House bill, but which I knew he would move to eliminate.

When he read off 117, I immediately (almost before he finished reading) said, "Mr. Chairman, I move the Senate agree with the House, namely that estate tax rates be reduced 5 percentage points in each year for four years, from 70 to 50."

When I made that motion, Rostenkowski protested, saying it could not be voted on until a discussion had been held and he would not entertain a motion to vote. I said, "Rosty, do you not remember two hours and 55 minutes ago you put your motion to a vote and denied any discussion?"

All in the room began to laugh.

I made the motion, and all the senators were unanimous in supporting me.

That is how the estate tax was reduced to 55 percent. The reason it didn't go to 50 percent was that after I retired from the Senate, Rostenkowski got the reduction stopped at 55, which it is now.

Rostenkowski's action on Item 52 gave me the example, and the opportunity, to do the same with Item 117.

Welfare Reform

*****

One of the most important issues to face the Congress in 1970 was President Nixon's proposal to reform the welfare system. I strongly favored welfare reform and looked forward to supporting the president's plan.

President Nixon submitted legislation drawn by one of his Democratic aides. It was referred to the Senate Finance Committee, of which I was a member. The committee spent most of the first half of the year 1970 holding public hearings on that important proposal.

Senator John J. Williams of Delaware, the senior Republican on the Finance Committee, took the lead role in analyzing that legislation. After spending many days and long hours questioning administration witnesses concerning the details of the welfare proposal, Senator Williams brought to light facts and figures that many senators found astonishing.

I joined Senator Williams in opposition to the proposed legislation.

The committee chairman, Russell Long of Louisiana, initially favorably disposed, as indeed was I, began to have doubts. The longer the committee hearings went on, the more skeptical Long became.

While no votes had been taken in the Finance Committee, there appeared to be considerable opposition to the president's plan.

During August and early September, Mr. Nixon vacationed at the California White House, his personal home at San Clemente.

Mr. Nixon was worried as to the attitude of the Finance Committee and requested several members to meet with him at San Clemente so he might get a better feel as to the details of the legislation.

He wanted to know why Williams, Byrd, and several others were so opposed, and why Long was so skeptical. He wanted a full discussion of his welfare legislation.

The president's plane, Air Force One, was put at the committee's disposal, but also taking along a number of White House aides whose presence Nixon needed in California.

From the committee there were the three ranking Democrats, Long of Louisiana, Abraham Ribicoff of Connecticut, and Byrd of Virginia. On the Republican side there were Wallace Bennett of Utah, Paul Fannin of Arizona, and Jack Miller of Iowa.

We flew to California on Sept. 2 and met with President Nixon at his San Clemente home the following morning. Those of us opposed to the legislation had an opportunity to present our reasons.

Russell Long, as committee chairman, led the discussion, saying he was undecided as to how he would vote. In leading the discussion, Long, at one point, said, "Mr. President, we are not concerned about the cost." I interrupted, saying, "Mr. President, I don't like to interrupt Senator Long, but I want to make clear I am one senator who is greatly concerned about the cost."

(Senator Long told that story many times.)

The legislation the president espoused was complicated and there were many reasons to oppose it. But Senator Williams' interrogations established two facts which brought about the bill's defeat:

One, it would have doubled the number of people on welfare, and, two, it would have doubled the cost.

Senator Long became a strong opponent, and the bill went down in defeat.

In addition to enhancing my role in the death of a bad piece of legislation, the invitation to meet with the President in California boosted my campaign.

Historically, campaigns begin the first week in September. The President also invited the six Finance Committee members, including myself, to be his guests at a formal state dinner he was giving in San Diego for the President of Mexico.

So at the starting point of the campaign, I had not one but two invitations from the Republican president.

This greatly upset my Republican opponents in Virginia.

Lewis F. Powell Jr.

❋❋❋❋

Lewis Powell and I were longtime friends. He was an outstanding lawyer, outstanding not only in Richmond but nationally, having been elected president of the American Bar Association.

We first worked together in my father's campaign for re-election to the U. S. Senate in 1946. Lewis was considered the brains of the "Democrats for Eisenhower" in 1952.

While I was not a part of that group, I worked with him in other campaigns through the years. When I announced on March 17, 1970 that I would seek re-election to the Senate as an Independent, Lewis came to my Senate office. He said he wanted me re-elected, but thought I could not win without a political party behind me. He urged that I seek the Republican nomination.

We talked for more than two hours and I explained to him my strategy and expressed conviction that I could win as an Independent, and would run as an Independent.

I walked with him to his car. When there he said I had convinced him that I knew what I was doing and he would help me in any way he could. Weeks later he became part of a small executive committee chaired by the outgoing Democratic governor, Mills E. Godwin Jr.

Lewis had a keen political mind, and was very helpful.

A year prior to that Richard M. Nixon became President of the United States. I had known Dick since he became a U. S. senator in 1951; I saw a great deal of him when he became vice president of the United States in 1953.

Shortly after he became president in 1969, he invited me to his office for a one-on-one talk, and volunteered that should I need anything from his administration I should go directly to him.

Following our personal and highly satisfactory discussion, he introduced me to his national security advisor; it was then that I first met Henry Kissinger.

Even before there was a vacancy on the Supreme Court, I began to talk with the president and his attorney general, John Mitchell, urging the appointment of Lewis Powell. Each was non-committal.

Months later, the attorney general invited four or five senators to dine with him aboard the presidential yacht. I was seated next to Attorney General Mitchell and used that occasion to talk with him again about Lewis Powell and the Supreme Court.

It was then, and for the first time, he spoke frankly, saying that both he and the president wanted to appoint a much younger person than Lewis, who was then 63.

I told John Mitchell that, as a general rule I concurred, but in this case I thought it could be waived because of what I considered Lewis' unique qualifications.

I said, however, I would cease and desist in urging Lewis' appointment. I let the matter drop.

When a vacancy occurred, the President appointed a highly respected federal judge from North Carolina. The Senate refused to confirm him and his nomination was withdrawn. A federal judge from Florida was then nominated. He, too, was refused confirmation by the Senate, as not having adequate qualifications.

It was then that Attorney General Mitchell phoned me to say the next nominee for the court must be one who can be confirmed. He said if the president decided to appoint Lewis Powell, could I assure the president that the Senate would confirm him. I told him I felt absolutely certain that if Lewis Powell were appointed he would be confirmed.

The next phone call from John Mitchell was to my apartment. He asked my wife, Gretchen, to tell me that the President had decided to appoint "my man." (He phrased it that way to flatter me; he knew as well as I that Lewis was his own man.)

At that point, there were two vacancies on the court and the President appointed, simultaneously,

William H. Rehnquist, who later became chief justice, and Lewis Powell.

The morning after these appointments were announced by the president on television, the attorney general telephoned me and said, "Now that the President has appointed your man, will you go to work for him?" I said, "Of course I will."

He then asked, "What do you want Lewis to do?" I said, ask him to come to my office at 10 a.m. two days hence. In the meantime I made appointments with as many members of the Judiciary Committee as I could reach.

On the appointed day, I first took Lewis to meet individually with the members of the committee, which must first approve his nomination. After that I took him from office to office to meet other senators. About 3 p.m., Lewis said, "We haven't had any lunch." I replied, "Lewis, we don't have time for lunch." Lewis insisted he needed at least a glass of milk.

So we then went to the cafeteria, and afterwards began seeing other senators, until Lewis said, "We have been going back and forth between two Senate office buildings, and I'm getting very tired."

Only then did it occur to me that there was an easier way.

I arranged to get the vice president's ceremonial office, right off from the Senate floor, where I put

Lewis, and brought senators there to meet him.

That venue speeded the process, but by 6:30 p.m. Lewis said, "I just can't go on any longer. I can hardly stand up." I said, "If you will just give me one more hour, we can get five or six more senators." He demurred so vehemently that I let the matter drop.

But from that morning until somewhere around 6:30 in the evening, in that eight-hour span, I had introduced Lewis to 61 senators.

It was a good day's work. I detected no problem.

After full Senate hearings, the Virginian was approved 89 to 1.

Jimmy Carter

I served in the U.S. Senate during five presidential administrations: Lyndon Johnson, Richard Nixon,
Gerald Ford, Jimmy Carter, and Ronald Reagan.

I had an unusually fine rapport with all except
Jimmy Carter. In talking with my colleagues, I found
that most shared my experience with President Carter.

Although Jimmy Carter served in the Georgia
Senate, and later as Governor of Georgia, when he became President of the United States he apparently made
little effort to develop friendships among the members
of the legislative branch of government.

He was the Democratic nominee for President in
1976, the same year I was seeking re-election to my
third term in the U.S. Senate, this time as an
Independent. Jimmy Carter came to Virginia twice that
election year and urged the voters to defeat me for re-
election.

I did not take offense because I knew politics well
enough to know that it was only logical that he should
support the Democratic nominee that year, Admiral
Elmo Zumwalt.

So, when he became president I made several
friendly speeches, speaking well of him. I determined

that I would cooperate with him in any way I could.

While I was elected as an Independent, I sat with the Democrats and voted with them in organizing the Senate. When President Carter wrote Democratic senators as to how he wanted to handle federal judgeships, which must be confirmed by the Senate, he wrote me the same letter.

The hand-written letter asked me, in regard to federal judgeships, to appoint a commission to determine the five best qualified individuals, then letting him take his choice among the five.

I responded promptly that I agreed with him that the best way to take politics out of the appointment of federal judges was appointment of such a commission. I told him I would do just that, and submit five names to him from whom he could choose to appoint, and I would pledge to support whomever he chose.

I did precisely as President Carter asked. My appointed commission was chaired by retired Congressman Thomas Downing of Newport News; one of its members was an African American lawyer from Norfolk.

Months later when the commission reported its five recommendations, I sent the report to the president and pledged again my support in the confirmation process for whomever he chose.

Months went by; I heard nothing from the White

House. Finally, Attorney General Griffin Bell came to my office. He said the president was not satisfied with the five names I submitted and wanted me to call the commission back into session and submit an additional name.

I told Attorney General Bell I could not do that as it would not be fair to Tom Downing and the other members of his commission – or to the five persons selected as the best qualified.

A couple of weeks later, the attorney general came for the second time to my office. We had another half-hour's talk. He said the president was waiting for my five recommendations.

I said I had already submitted those names. But, he said the president could not accept them. He needed to have the name of a black on the list. I said, that was news to me. I didn't know anything about such a request and showed him the letter I had received from the president asking me to get the "best qualified."

I asked Griffin Bell, "Wouldn't you agree that I did exactly what the President asked me to do?" He said he agreed that I had – but "he's the President."

He came again for a third and then a fourth time, and each time I told him it wouldn't be fair to the commission or to the five already deemed "the best qualified." I did exactly what the president asked me to do – "get the best qualified."

So, again I refused to change the five recommendations, which gave the president complete discretion to choose any of the five.

Again, for the fifth time, the attorney general came to see me, saying the president was dissatisfied with my list and expected me to submit a new list.

He then added that the president had made a commitment before the election to Martin Luther King Sr., Coretta Scott King, and Mayor Tom Bradley of Los Angeles to appoint a black federal judge in every Southern state. I said again, as I had many times, that I followed precisely what he asked me to do and I would not change the list of the "best qualified."

The purpose of President Carter's letter to the senators was, according to Mr. Carter, to take politics out of judicial appointments. But we found he was knee-deep in judicial politics, even before he was elected president.

By the sixth time Griffin Bell visited me, it was embarrassing to him and to me, so he finally said he had done all he could. Would I mind, he asked, if the President called me? I said I would be delighted to talk with him anytime.

By then it was August. The Congress was in recess and I was at my office in Winchester on a Saturday. I answered the phone.

It was the White House saying the President apologized for calling me during the recess, but he was anxious to talk with me and asked if I would come to the White House to meet with him.

I said, tell the president I will meet with him anytime, any place.

We set a date for a few days hence. I drove to Washington and when I was ushered into the Oval Office, the President was most gracious in greeting me, even having two photographers present – not the usual one but two. They took a lot of photos.

We sat down and President Carter said he wanted to talk with me about the judgeship matter. (Of course, I already knew what he wanted to talk about.) He said of the 55 Democratic senators, Attorney General Bell had "made a deal" (that's the word he used) with all except me. The president said that I, Byrd, was the only senator he was required to discuss the matter with.

When he finished, I told him I followed his letter precisely and had no personal interest in any of the five – and would support whomever he chose.

After considerable discussion, without any change of attitude on the part of the president or me, he said, "Well now, I want you to understand my position. I promised Martin Luther King Sr., Coretta King and Mayor Bradley that I would appoint a black federal judge in every Southern state. So, I have to fulfill that commitment to them."

Replying, I said, "Mr. President, I feel you made a commitment to me. Following your letter, I did exactly what you asked me to do. I don't know what other commitments you made, but I feel you made a commitment to me."

The meeting ended when I would not change my position and he wouldn't change his.

We did not end on the friendliest of terms.

In September, after the congressional recess and the Congress had returned, Attorney General Bell came to see me for the seventh time. He came to tell me that they had "scoured" (his own word) the state and found a black who might be able to get confirmed.

I told him I would not support anyone who was not on the "best-qualified" list.

The president submitted the name of a Richmond lawyer who told me he understood my position, but did hope that I could introduce him to the Senate Judiciary Committee, saying it would be embarrassing for him if his state's senator would not do so.

I told him I would do so, but would tell the committee what I had said all along: I would oppose anyone NOT on the best-qualified list of the Downing Commission.

Fast forward.

I did present him to the committee, but said I would oppose his confirmation, and stated my reasons.

Then, a real shocker, both to me and to the nominee.

The chairman said there had been charges made against the nominee which must be examined by the committee. He gave the nominee the option of testifying that day or at a later date. The nominee was clearly surprised, as was I. It was obvious that he didn't know what to do or say.

After thinking about it two or three minutes, he said he would prefer the hearing be held at a later date. That ended the judgeship saga. The nominee did not seek another hearing.

The judgeship remained vacant until Ronald Reagan became president.

Nixon Resignation

————————— ✳✳✳✳ —————————

Probably the most dramatic moment in my political life was Aug. 8, 1973.

President Nixon had been impeached by the U. S. House of Representatives and was to be tried by the Senate. His conviction was a near certainty. Indeed, old friends and supporters, including myself, were prepared to vote against him.

The White House telephoned my Senate office asking if I would go to the White House at 7:00 that night. I was there promptly and the staff took me, with eight or nine other senators and 15 or 18 members of the House of Representatives, into the Cabinet room.

I was seated in the vice president's chair directly across from the President. The president's chair is always at the middle of the table, not at the end.

President Nixon came in sharply at 8 p.m. He took his seat and started talking. He said, "I called you here to tell you personally what I am gong to do when I speak to the American people by television tonight.

"I want to tell each of you personally because without your help I would not have been able to end the Vietnam war nor bring balance to the Supreme Court. Within a few minutes after leaving you, I will speak to the American people, telling them I will resign as president effective noon tomorrow."

President Nixon is the only president in our history to resign. He talked about his family. He recalled political events important to him. President Nixon spoke of friendships and old times, but not mentioning any of us by name.

It was amazing – the most powerful man in the world telling us he was going to resign his presidency. He spoke to us in the Cabinet room for exactly 30 minutes, stopping precisely at 8:30. No one else said a word.

He ended by saying "I hope....I hope....I hope....I hope I haven't let you down."

With those words he drew his hankerchief, wiped his eyes and left the room. I turned to the senator next to me and said, "How in the world can he possibly go on national television?"

At 9:00 at the White House, we watched him on television as he spoke to the American people, without giving the least hint of the emotional visit just 30 minutes earlier.

At 2:00 the next morning, the phone rang in our Washington apartment. My wife awakened me, and I said, "Tell them to call in the morning." She said, "It's the President."

President Nixon asked me if I thought he had

done the right thing. I said, "Mr. President, under the circumstances, I feel what you did was appropriate."

We had a nice talk and he invited me to visit him in California, saying he would never return to Washington.

Subsequently, former President Nixon did return to Washington on several occasions and asked that I be present at each small gathering.

Johnson's Nominee For Chief Justice

✳✳✳✳

Regardless of how many times one has attended White House dinners, they are always impressive, and so it was on the evening of June 4, 1968.

President Lyndon Johnson and I were one seat apart. Between us was the wife of the guest of honor, a South American president. She spoke only Spanish.

So the President and I spent most of the dinner talking with each other. We were longtime friends and had much in common, but not always on the same page politically.

Toward the end of the dinner, President Johnson leaned closer to me and said, "Harry, I will be out of office in seven months, but before I leave I want to do something for you. What do you want?"

I said, "I am grateful to you, Mr. President, and grateful for your friendship, but there is nothing I want." (Being able to say "there is nothing I want" are to me the sweetest words one could ever say in Washington.)

President Johnson persisted, saying, "What about a judgeship?" I replied that I had recommended someone for the federal vacancy in Virginia, saying "he is an excellent lawyer with judicial temperament, his name is ..." The president put up his hand, "I don't care about his name; if you want him, then I want him."

"Here is what you do," he continued, "call my Attorney General (Ramsey Clark). He isn't worth a damn, but tell him I want your man appointed." I thanked the President.

At 3 o'clock the next morning the phone rang at my Washington residence. It was my close friend, D. Lathan Mims, who gave me the news that Sen. Robert Kennedy had been shot and killed in California. Kennedy was seeking the Democratic presidential nomination.

This tragic event threw all of Washington into turmoil, especially the Justice Department.

I reasoned it was not the time to be talking with the Attorney General about a judgeship.

I let time pass and then called one of the president's assistants. I told him of the dinner conversation, asked him to check the accuracy of my statement with the president, and suggested it would be best if the White House were to tell the attorney general of the president's wishes in regard to the judgeship. The White House phoned later to say all of this had been done.

On June 26, another event occurred: President Johnson nominated Abe Fortas, then an Associate Justice, to be Chief Justice of the United States. This, of course, required Senate confirmation. I immediately recognized that this put me on the hot seat in regard to the federal judgeship in Virginia.

I had hoped to vote for the Fortas nomination for many reasons, among which were my desire to give support to Lyndon Johnson. My feeling was that it would be appreciated in the Jewish community, for which I had a high regard and which consistently had given me good support, and, thirdly, I felt it could help stem the loss of support among Democratic activists feeling unhappy about some of my votes.

A yes vote on Fortas, I thought, could be a political plus.

I set about to study his judicial record. But the more I studied it, the more concerned I became.

After giving it much thought, I reached the conclusion I could not cast my vote to confirm Fortas. In addition, I felt I must make a carefully prepared Senate speech making clear my reasons.

I telephoned Alex Harman of Pulaski, my nominee for the federal judgeship in Virginia, and told him what I felt I had to do, and if I did make such a speech it would jeopardize, if not kill, his appointment.

I appreciated and never forgot Alex's reply: "I would like to be a federal judge, and believe I would be a good one. But if you believe the confirmation of Fortas as Chief Justice of the United States would not be in the best interests of our country, I accept your decision. My disappointment is not adequate reason to go against your best judgment on a matter of such great importance."

(Several years later, my longtime friend, Gov. Mills E. Godwin Jr., appointed Alex to the Supreme Court of Virginia.)

I spoke in the Senate on Sept. 9, 1968, three months and five days after the White House dinner. It was a lengthy speech. I felt the Senate had a deep obligation to go carefully into the Fortas record as an associate justice. Once a nominee is confirmed by the Senate, assuming the nominee's good behavior, there are no checks or restraints on his lifetime appointment. Fortas had been confirmed as associate justice by voice vote without opposition.

As an associate justice, Mr. Fortas became a key player in what I regarded as the excesses of the court under Earl Warren as chief justice.

The nomination of Mr. Justice Fortas was submitted on June 26. Many of my colleagues argued that because President Johnson announced on March 31 that he would not be a candidate for re-election, he, therefore, was a "lame duck" president and should not submit nominations for the federal judiciary.

I did not agree with such a view.

Every president continues to have the power and

the responsibilities of his office until the hour he relinquishes it to his successor. John Marshall, perhaps the most famous of all the top justices, was appointed only days before John Adams relinquished the presidency to Thomas Jefferson, a political opponent of Marshall.

When does a president become a "lame duck" insofar as submitting nominations is concerned? Seven months before he leaves office, 14 months, or four years? Bear in mind that the Constitution now prevents a president from serving more than two terms. So any president who begins his second term automatically is barred from seeking re-election.

I put little credence in the arguments of those who said President Johnson should not, seven months before the end of his term, submit a nomination for the Supreme Court.

The Senate's responsibility, as I saw it, "is to meet the issue head-on, to deal squarely with the qualifications and the philosophy of the appointee..."

In my Senate speech, I quoted liberally from various Supreme Court justices. I expressed the view that appointees should possess the qualities of justices like Oliver Wendell Holmes, Louis D. Brandeis, Charles Evans Hughes, Harlan Fiske Stone, Benjamin H. Cardozo, and Felix Frankfurter.

I reflected the view of Mr. Justice Cardozo that "justices are not commissioned to make and unmake rules at pleasure, in accordance with changing views of expediency or wisdom." I maintained that a majority of the Warren Court had consistently done precisely this.

I quoted Mr. Justice Frankfurter, who contended that the court should not repudiate "the experience of our whole past in asserting destructively novel judicial power."

Earlier, Mr. Justice Frankfurter warned against such action:

"The court's authority – possessed of neither the purse nor the sword – ultimately rests on sustained public confidence in its moral sanction. Such feeling must be nourished by the Court's complete detachment ... from political entanglements..."

In my speech to the Senate, I said the Supreme Court needed to be brought into balance, that under Mr. Warren it had become an extremist court. A majority, which usually included Mr. Fortas, had taken the court to the far left.

I concluded my speech with an unequivocal summary of my objection to the nominee:

"During the time Mr. Fortas has been a member of this Court, he has established himself as a disciple of Chief Justice Warren and has embraced wholeheartedly the Warren philosophy.

"If I were to vote to elevate him to the position of chief justice, I would be voting to give him the authority to influence decisions by assigning cases to other justices to write opinions, and the authority to assign judges and retired judges to circuit and district courts throughout the nation.

"If I were to support the confirmation of Mr. Justice Fortas to the position of chief justice, I would be voting to promote a member of the Court who had embraced, and become a part of, the Warren philosophy – a philosophy that decrees that the Court may cast legal precedent aside when it does not square with personal desires of the judges.

"If I were to cast my vote for Mr. Justice Fortas, I would be placing my stamp of approval on the extreme leftist trend of the Warren court, a trend to which Mr. Justice Fortas apparently has dedicated himself...

"Were I to vote to ratify the nomination of Mr. Justice Fortas to be chief justice, I would be voting to perpetuate, in the key judicial position in our nation, the Warren philosophy.

"As one who feels the Warren court has done great damage to our nation – to the future welfare of our people – how can I vote to confirm as chief justice one who proclaims the Warren era the greatest in Court history; not only proclaims it in words, but by deeds, namely, by his decisions as associate justice?

"That Mr. Warren and Mr. Fortas were determined to perpetuate the centralization of power in

Washington was dramatized by Chief Justice Warren's statement in press interviews that if the nomination of Mr. Fortas was not confirmed, he, Mr. Warren, would continue to serve."

I pointed out that by thus conditioning his retirement, Mr. Warren was telling the Senate, "either you take my preference as a successor or I won't retire." I suggested the Senate would not want to be so coerced.

Senate opposition intensified with each passing day and Fortas' nomination was withdrawn on Oct. 4, 1968. Johnson, Fortas and Warren had lost the battle. That ended the president's interest in the federal judgeship in Virginia.

I debated with myself whether to talk with the president again regarding Alex Harman. I decided to do so 30 days before Johnson's term expired, because it

President Lyndon Johnson and Senator Byrd were close friends, although the two did not see eye to eye politically on many issues.

was Johnson who had volunteered support for my nominee.

I was cordially received by the president when we met in the Oval Office.

As we sat down the president started talking, looking around the room as if he were talking to himself: "I don't understand the Senate. I served there and was majority leader, but I still don't get it. Abe Fortas would have made a great chief justice. I don't get it, I don't understand the Senate."

Then abruptly he turned his attention to me and said, "What is it you want to talk with me about?"

Of course, he knew the answer to that question; and, of course, I did not comment on his ruminations about the Senate and Fortas.

I recalled for him our dinner conversation of the past June.

He quickly replied: "Of course, I remember our conversation. The problem is the attorney general and your Virginia colleague (William Spong of Portsmouth) want someone else. I want your man."

My reply was brief: "If you are with me, Mr. President, it doesn't make much difference who the attorney general wants or who Spong wants."

Then he jumped out of his chair and said, "Follow me." With a quick walk to the next office he spoke loudly to his assistant:

"You telephone my attorney general and tell him I want Senator Byrd's man appointed to the Virginia judgeship."

I thanked him, we shook hands, and said goodbye.

I was not surprised, however, that nothing subsequently happened. The federal judgeship in Virginia remained vacant until Richard Nixon became President.

The Fortas nomination and my part in it was one of various political events that led to what became Virginia's politically historic year of 1970.

Senator Byrd served in the United States Senate with five Presidents and has known many more. He is pictured above with President Ronald Reagan. Former Virginia Governor Mills Godwin, a close Byrd friend, is pictured at right.

The photo below was taken during a visit by former Senator Byrd to the White House during the Presidency of George H.W. Bush.

Associated Press

✳✳✳✳

The Associated Press is the nation's largest news-gathering organization.

Its staff, headquartered in New York City, is governed by an 18-member board of directors elected by the 1,600 members of the cooperative. Terms are three years with the proviso that no person could serve more than three consecutive terms.

I have been on a number of boards, but the most interesting by far was that of the Associated Press. I was elected to the board of directors in 1950.

Its 18 newspaper publishers are from throughout the nation.

The chairman at that time was the publisher of the Philadelphia Bulletin. Among other members were the publishers of The New York Times, The Los Angeles Times, Dallas Morning News, Washington Evening Star, and Louisville Courier Journal.

In 1951, President Truman, on April 11, relieved General Douglas MacArthur of his duties as commander of the American army in Korea. When McArthur returned to the United States he was invited to address the Congress.

The AP board, holding its April meeting in New

York, recessed to watch the speech on television.

I sat on a small bench with Roy Roberts, the 250-pound editor of the Kansas City Star and a leader of the Republican Party in the Midwest.

The MacArthur speech was one of the general's best, he undoubtedly hoping it would ignite a fire propelling him toward the Republican presidential nomination.

When the General concluded his address with "Old soldiers never die, they just fade away," it was a tremendous hit with the Congress.

It made an even greater hit with my board colleague, with whom I was sitting. Roy had tears rolling down his cheeks and kept saying "A magnificent speech. A wonderful speech. It's just what this country needs."

I said, "Roy, you seem deeply affected. Let me ask you this: You are regarded as perhaps the most important leader of the Republican party in the Midwest. If General MacArthur seeks the Republican presidential nomination, what would be your attitude?"

He still had his handkerchief in his hand. He thought a few moments, wiped his eyes again, and said, "I would vote against the son-of-a bitch."

Moods can change quickly.

Another AP event, of a different type, was in October of 1956. At the end of the first day of the board meeting, one of the members, speaking to no one in particular, said it was too bad we didn't think about trying to get some World Series tickets, the New York Yankees playing the Brooklyn Dodgers. He added, of course, "It's too late now."

Don Maxwell, the editor of the Chicago Tribune, spoke up, saying he might be able to get some tickets. How many did we need? With the members and their wives it would be 36 tickets. Everyone laughed.

The next morning on the board table were 36 tickets in pairs face down. Each member filed by, taking a pair. The two seats I obtained were situated right behind, and almost a part of, the Yankee dugout.

It was that day that Don Larsen pitched his perfect game - no HITS, no RUNS, no ERRORS, no MEN ALLOWED ON BASE. Larsen pitched a total of only 97 balls over nine innings.

I was elected to the board in 1950. The following year Reuters, the great British news gathering organization dating back to 1851, held a dinner in London to commemorate its 100th anniversary.

Paul Miller, president of the Gannett newspapers, and I, both being AP directors, attended as representatives of the AP. In connection with that trip, Paul and I worked out an arrangement where I would file special articles for the 14 Gannett newspapers as well as my two newspapers, The Winchester Star and the Daily

News-Record in Harrisonburg. I planned eight weeks in Europe.

Since I would be in London for the Reuters dinner, I immediately began trying to arrange an interview with Winston Churchill.

For several weeks – even after I arrived in London – I heard nothing from Mr. Churchill's office. When it did call, it set a date for me to see Mr. Churchill on which I was committed to be in Scotland at a dinner being given in honor of my wife and me by a friend we had met aboard the Queen Mary en route to England.

I explained this to Mr. Churchill's secretary and said I would rather have an audience with the great British prime minister than anyone in the whole world. But the planned dinner was only two nights away. I would feel like a heel to tell the host and hostess that I had something better to do and could not keep the dinner engagement.

I telephoned Paul Miller to tell him I had the interview with Churchill, but could not keep it .

Paul exploded.

"You are fired – now and forever. What a damn fool thing to turn down an interview with perhaps the most important man in the world, an interview which almost every journalist is seeking but can't get."

I calmed him down a little bit – but not much – by telling him I was working with Mr. Churchill's secre-

tary to change, hopefully, the meeting at the House of
Commons to another day. Fortunately, it worked out –
so Paul and I lived happily ever after.

(For an account of that interview, see page 112.)

An Interview With Winston Churchill

――――――――✷✷✷✷――――――――

For more than a century, citizens of the Shenandoah Valley have taken a great interest and a great pride in the military campaigns of Gen. Stonewall Jackson. Winchester and its five battles hold an important place in the history of the War Between the States. Local historians and many from afar have studied Jackson's campaigns in much detail.

But, of my acquaintances, the one who knew it best, the one who could cite facts and figures and times and places and interpret spontaneously the tactical reasons behind Jackson's maneuvers was one who never set foot in the Shenandoah Valley. That man was Winston Churchill.

Mr. Churchill was a guest in the home of my mother and father in 1929 when my father was Governor of Virginia. The British statesman used our home in Richmond as headquarters while he studied the Civil War battlefields to the east and south of the former Confederate capital.

Twenty-two years would go by before I saw him again.

It was the summer of 1951 on the eve of his second election as Britain's prime minister that I spent four delightful hours with him at his office at the House of Commons. I was doing some newspaper work in Europe at the time, filing stories for the New York-based Gannett newspapers, as well as for The Winchester Star and the Harrisonburg Daily News-Record.

It was 2 p.m. when I entered Mr. Churchill's office – and it was nearly an hour later before the English statesman stopped talking about the Shenandoah Valley and the American Civil War.

During that 45-50 minutes, Mr. Churchill told me more about the history of the area in which I lived all my life than I had ever known – and more about the details and purposes and tactics of Stonewall Jackson's Valley Campaign than ever had come to my attention.

All of Mr. Churchill's monologue was spontaneous. What he had to say he said with relish, with glee – and with great enthusiasm. His discourse was not only stimulating but fascinating. I kept thinking to myself, why did I know so little about the great events which took place on virtually the same soil on which I trod for nearly 36 years?

(As an aside, I might say that during the entire time I was with him he was slowly sipping a tumbler of brandy; he didn't offer me any.)

Mr. Churchill finally left the subjects of the Civil

War, the Shenandoah Valley, and Stonewall Jackson, during which time I had said practically nothing. We then began to discuss the topics of the day and government philosophy, but not before Mr. Churchill asserted he hoped to visit the Shenandoah Valley and its battlefields before he died. That was not to be.

The year 1951 was the 100th anniversary of Reuters, the British News Agency. Mrs. Byrd and I attended the gala dinner celebrating the centennial, which the Queen attended. Mr. Churchill, having been a foreign correspondent himself, notably during the Boer war, had a keen interest in journalism and indeed for a while made a living by the pen.

During 1951 there was much dissatisfaction in the United States with President Truman. He was at a low point in his presidency. That prompted me to say to Mr. Churchill that it seemed to me that the British Parliamentary system – where the leader of government could be changed within a short span of a few weeks – had much to commend it over the American system.

I shall never forget Mr. Churchill's reply: "Ah yes, Mr. Byrd, but don't forget this: that the great strength of the American system is that the 48 states acting through their own legislatures can to a very considerable degree resolve their own local problems." And then he added: "You in America are not centralized like we are in England."

Never had I heard such an eloquent appraisal of States Rights. I was fascinated that a great world statesman 3,000 miles from our shores should recognize and proclaim what so many Americans at that time did not, and even now do not, realize – the dangers of a government too highly centralized, something Thomas Jefferson warned against 150 years earlier.

What a fascinating person Winston Churchill was. He was elected to Parliament at age 26. Before he was 30, he sought to dominate the senior members of Parliament and to lecture the prime minister.

Before the age of 40 he had held various cabinet posts and, as the first Lord of the Admiralty during World War I, he formulated and executed the Dardanelles campaign, which for England and its allies proved a disaster. This ended his meteoric rise.

With only a short lapse, he was consistently re-elected a member of the House of Commons, but for most of the next 25 years his was a lonely voice and one which was not often heeded. He served longer in a freely elected parliamentary body than any person in history, from 1901 until his death in 1965, excepting a two-year period, 1922-24.

In discussing the House of Commons and the British government, Mr. Churchill recalled that the historic House of Parliament had been severely damaged by German bombs during World War II. In rebuilding, he said his colleagues wanted to enlarge and modernize the chamber. Mr. Churchill allowed, however, that he "persevered" (to use his own word) until Parliament was restored in precisely its original form.

He said he would like to give me two pieces of advice, should I ever have occasion to build a legislative chamber. First, he said, it should not be semi-circular like we have in the United States; it should be oblong, putting one party on one side and the other party on the other side – and make them stay there. I didn't remind him that he himself had changed parties several times.

The second piece of advice was this: Never have a legislative chamber large enough to seat all the members; make them pile in, sit on the floor, or sit on each other's lap. He deemed it much more democratic that way. After a pause, he added, "And, besides, it is much easier to speak to a crowded chamber."

What immediately went through my mind was that the man whose eloquence did so much to rally the English people during their darkest hours of World War II was thinking not so much as an architect but as an orator, of which he was one of England's greatest.

During my interview with Mr. Churchill, Mrs. Byrd waited for me in the outer office. When I introduced the British leader to her, he asked whether either of us had been through the House of Commons. Neither had. Mr. Churchill then said, "I'll give you a personally conducted tour."

With the three of us alone in the House of Commons, I vowed that this personally conducted tour would remain one of the most cherished events of my life. Even now, nearly 60 years later, it still is.

Interview And Correspondence
With Spanish Dictator

✳✳✳✳

In 1954, I spent five weeks in Europe interviewing various heads of government, reporting for the Gannett newspapers and for my two.

I found Prime Minister Antonio de O Salazar of Portugal to be tremendously interesting on a subject in which I had much interest.

Salazar was an economics professor until he became Portugal's dictator. He was a quiet and studious individual, and gracious to a high degree, even personally seeing me to my car.

He demanded his government balance its budget each year. I didn't see a single photo of him throughout Lisbon.

What a difference it was a few days later when I met with Spain's dictator, Gen. Francisco Franco. Photos of him were everywhere, seemingly on every street in Madrid.

The night before my appointment, a representative of the Spanish state department wanted to know just what questions I planned to ask the general. I demurred, and changed the subject.

Again, the next morning in taking me to the

palace, the state department official asked what I planned to discuss. I again passed it off, by filibustering a bit. The Spaniard volunteered that I should not mention Tito, the dictator of Yugoslavia.

I kept that in the back of my mind for use at the appropriate time.

My conversation with Franco was through an interpreter. Early on I mentioned that I had a visit with his counterpart in Portugal. Franco laughed and said, "Ah, Salazar. You know what I tell Salazar. I say, 'Salazar, you don't act enough like a dictator.'" Both of us got a good laugh out of that.

I had three key questions I wanted to ask Franco. After getting replies to those, I did exactly what the state department official told me not to do.

I said, "General, my government just recently made an arrangement with Marshal Tito in Yugoslavia; we have military bases in Spain. Does this mean you, Tito, and the United States are allies?

Franco reacted immediately, partially rising from his chair, saying, "I'll tell you about Tito. He came to Spain during our civil war and fought against me."

That mention of Tito really set the Spanish dictator into spirited discussion. I kept throwing Tito questions. For more than an hour, I got a vivid report on the Spanish Civil War. It was the winning of that war that brought about his dictatorship.

He even brought Winston Churchill into the conversation, telling me that Gibraltar really belonged to Spain, but that Spain would not be able to get it so long as Churchill lived.

We seemed to hit it off nicely and I continued by corresponding with him when I returned home.

On April 30, 1956, I wrote the leader of Spain the following letter:

"During the past several weeks I have talked with a number of influential Americans who seem to be taking seriously the new anti-Stalin line enunciated by the Kremlin leaders. The impression seems to be gaining that Communist Russia is turning over a new leaf.

"I am not prepared to subscribe to such a view. I am impressed with the facts on Communism you developed in your talk with me in July 1954. You also brought out a point that Americans then did not realize: that the break between the Soviets and Yugoslavia was actually a break between two individuals, Tito and Stalin.

"Many of us in America would be tremendously interested in your analysis of the new Russian maneuvers. Anti-Communists must be careful not to be fooled by Soviet propaganda.

"Would you be inclined to write me your views and permit me to disseminate them in this country? Most of our people are baffled as to just what Russia's new look really means.

"I am delighted that Spain is now in the United Nations."

In a letter to me dated June 25, 1956, the general responded. The letter, as published in The New York Times, July 10, 1956, is printed below:

THE NEW YORK TIMES, JULY 10, 1956

FRANCO DECLARES SOVIET PERIL RISES - Anti-Stalin Drive is Shift in Tactics, Not Aim, Letter to Virginia Editor says.

Generalissimo Francisco Franco, Spanish Chief of State, warned today that the new Soviet policy constituted a "greater danger over a long period of time."

"The downgrading of Stalin does not represent any change in objectives," he said in a letter to Harry F. Byrd Jr., editor and publisher of The Winchester Star and the Harrisonburg Daily News-Record.

The anti-Stalin campaign, General Franco added, is just "a variation in tactical strategy to better attain these objectives."

Mr. Byrd, who two years ago had had a lengthy interview with the Spanish leader in Madrid, had recently sought his appraisal of the Soviet Union's "new look." The Franco letter appeared with a copyright article in today's issues of the two Virginia newspapers. Text of Letter - El Pardo Palace, June 25, 1956 - The Hon. Harry F. Byrd Jr.

Dear Friend:

I received your kind letter of April 30, in which you asked me for my opinion on the new anti-Stalin attitude which has been proclaimed by the leaders of the Kremlin. It is not difficult to see through their tactic: I believe, like yourself, that the present expression of Soviet policy does not represent any change in the objectives pursued, but rather a variation in tactical strategy to better attain these objectives; having tried some procedures, they put others into action which they judge more appropriate. The near future will confirm this. In any form, it constitutes a clear expression of the dynamism and agility of their policy.

The very grave accusations of Khrushchev (Nikita S. Khruschev, Soviet Community party chief) and the attendant publicity results from a complicated and difficult crisis in the Soviet policy. What else could justify permitting this very grave impact, which adversely affects the internal and external prestige of communism? They could have effected the change and justified what they call a new collective course as the crowning of some labor, as the end of one period and the beginning of another, without having to resort to making these extremely grave accusations public, and creating a havoc which adversely affects communism in general and which has been turned against them as accomplices and collaborators.

When they must defend themselves in this fashion, it is because somebody is attacking and attacking strongly.

Army's Role Discussed

It has been known for some time that the Communist leaders and the principal figures of the Communist party, like the generals and military leaders, felt themselves under the constant menace of Stalinist terrorism, with its periodic purges and shots in the back without any possible defense against them. Stalin's death brought them together with the aim of freeing themselves from this terror. In the process, the Army had to play a principal role. This explains its part in the new situation.

From the point of view of Communist foreign policy, the growing repudiation of subservience by the Communist parties of other nations to Moscow and Soviet imperialism made advisable rectification of a strategy which jeopardized the attainment of Communist expansion abroad. It became necessary to place the blame on someone to give a semblance of sincerity to the rectification. The immediate reconciliation with Tito (President Tito of Yugoslavia) demonstrates this.

Policy Bad For West

In the light of the foregoing, we must conclude that the change in tactics obeys internal needs of com-

munism, and we must deduce, as a result, that what they consider good must necessarily be bad for the West.

There are no other reasons which could justify (such) fundamental changes in a policy which has expanded their frontiers to unprecedented limits and which has permitted them to occupy one of the foremost places in the community of nations.

What is evident is that Russia today needs time and space to consolidate its conquests and its new internal situations, and it is to this that the new policy responds; to show themselves in sheep's clothing, attract attention and create problems in other areas, which, by permitting them to consolidate their situation, also permits them to assimilate what they have attained so far. Time is a powerful ally for them.

In brief: The letting up of the moment constitutes a greater danger over a long period of time. I am sure that you, who know Russia and the unchanging aims of Communist policy, will not be far from this point of view.

Very cordially yours,

F. Franco

This is the end of Franco's letter to me which was published in full in The New York Times.

We had additional correspondence of a more personal nature, Franco thanking me for all the "thoughtful attentiveness which I value all the more that it comes

from a person with whom I am united in sincere friendship."

Yugoslavia

✳✳✳✳

In 1954 Yugoslavia was governed by a communist dictatorship under Josip Broz Tito. He had broken with Communist Russia because of a disagreement with Josef Stalin, the Soviet dictator.

So, while Yugoslavia under Tito had a Communist government, it was to a considerable degree free from Russian domination.

I went there nine years after the ending of World War II to assess the economic and political conditions of a country governed by a Communist dictatorship but relatively free from the demands of the Soviet Union.

Mrs. Byrd and I drove from Trieste, Italy across the mountain to Zagreb, Yugoslavia. We spent the night there and the next day drove 240 miles to Belgrade. What impressed me greatly was in that 240 miles on the main highway of the country, we encountered only nine automobiles.

I found Yugoslavia to be a tight dictatorship.

The AP correspondent made appointments for me with some of the top government officials.

In each case in my conversations with those officials, I mentioned seeing only nine automobiles during that 240-mile drive. In each case my question was an-

126

swered with a question.

Why do people need automobiles? The only persons who need automobiles are those who run government-owned factories or government-owned businesses.

That gave the full flavor of a Communist state.

"Purest Democracy
Since Ancient Greece"

✳✳✳✳

In 1959 I went to Cuba three different times –
April, July and October.

It was Jan. 1 of that year that Fidel Castro took
over the Cuban government. He was 32 years old and
for six years had been training and organizing militia to
overthrow the Batista regime.

In doing newspaper work for The Winchester Star
and the Daily News-Record of Harrisonburg, I got an
early insight into the Cuban revolution.

I had the good luck of knowing Jules DuBois, the
Latin American correspondent of The Chicago Tribune.

He had known Castro in the mountains and had
written a favorable biography, but became critical when
Castro turned toward Communism. Castro began de-
nouncing DuBois on the radio and he soon became his
Public Enemy Number One.

In April, I lunched with two leading Cuban businessmen, large landowners. When I asked whether they
expected a leftward lurch by Castro, one responded,
"Don't worry about Fidel, we can take care of him."

In July when I returned to Cuba, I tried to locate
the two businessmen only to learn they had fled the

country, their property confiscated.

By my next trip there were thousands of workers out of jobs in Cuba. Private investment, necessary for growth in any free country, was at a standstill, reflecting widespread unemployment.

I was able to arrange an appointment with Dr. Rufo Lopez-Fresquet, Minister of Finance, who told me it would be necessary for the revolutionary government to "reorient the thinking of the businessmen."

The man who wants to "reorient the thinking of the businessmen" is considered the most "moderate" of the revolutionaries. Incidentally, I went through six guarded doors to reach his private office.

By my third trip in October, Fidel Castro had gone deeper into Communism. Jules and I listened to that violently anti-U.S. speech from the apartment of the editor of The Havana Times. Castro had brought 500,000 machete-bearing Cubans from the rural areas. His speech denounced DuBois almost as much as it did the United States.

When the crowd learned that Castro's Public Enemy Number One (Jules) was in the apartment house overlooking the palace grounds, our host shut off the electricity for the elevator and urged Jules and me not to leave his apartment until all attending the Castro rally had left.

Jules previously had been so threatened by a mob

that police went to his rescue. The small community of American correspondents felt DuBois's life was in danger. The Chicago Tribune was telephoned, urging that DuBois be recalled – which was done.

I felt no danger, but the Naval attache at the American Embassy felt that because I had spent so much time with Jules DuBois, it would be wise for me to leave Havana.

The Navy Captain drove me the 600 miles to Santiago, leaving before daylight and arriving after dark.

The following article, written by me in 1959, helps put Castro's Cuban revolution into perspective.

HAVANA, Cuba – Those who supplied much of the fuel for Fidel Castro's revolutionary movement are themselves feeling the heat, generated by the man they helped install.

The armed rebellion on this sugar island 90 miles off the American coast ended January 1 with the fleeing of Dictator Batista – but the revolutionary processes are just now beginning.

The leaders of the Castro movement which began six years ago were those of the Castro type – young intellectuals – strongly assisted by the professional and business interests. The industrial workers and the farm laborers took little part – or sided with Batista.

It was a revolution not of the downtrodden but

rather of the prosperous. Those in the middle economic bracket wanted for Cuba more democracy and less corruption.

Revolt of Prosperous

To the businessman, the professional man and the university professor, the Castro movement represented a means of ridding Cuba of Batista's fantastic graft and corruption.

Reliable estimates put Batista's personal take at $100 million. His top officials are credited with siphoning from the national treasury, or from the pay-offs, fortunes ranging from a few million dollars to $65 million. And this in a nation with an annual budget of $400 million, roughly the size of Virginia's.

What is the situation today?

Dictator Batista has been replaced by Fidel Castro, the latter's power being as absolute as was the former's.

Corruption in government has been eliminated. No longer is it possible for lawyers to settle their cases by private payments to judges.

And now if one million dollars is appropriated for a certain government project, that amount is so spent. (Previously no more than 75 per cent customarily found its way into the project for which it was appropriated.)

But this does not mean democracy has come to Cuba. It hasn't.

There will be no free elections, Castro says, for at least four years.

There is no legislature.

Government is by decree, and Castro's system is a free-wheeling one – he and his associates playing both the political and economic game by ear.

The base for Fidel Castro's support has changed drastically. Widespread opposition to Batista brought to Castro the support of intellectuals, business and professional men who wanted an end to government corruption.

Many Disenchanted

Most of these have become disenchanted – and many fearful – while Castro himself has been directing his appeal to the farm laborer and to the industrial worker.

To the former he has promised land reform (free land taken from someone else) and to the latter he has decreed a reduction in rents, telephone charges, and the like.

To dramatize his strength and his popularity, Dr. Castro had 500,000 agricultural workers converge on Havana, bringing with them their machetes, large razor-sharp knives used for cutting sugar cane.

Most who came were in their early twenties; more than half could neither read nor write; few had any part in the revolution but all are deeply swayed by the emo-

tional appeal of Castro's speeches, which are long and many.

The demonstration was a political success; and a warning to his opponents.

Castro Power Absolute

Today, seven months after assuming power, Fidel Castro is in full command of Cuba. His power is absolute. One businessman after another told me: "Castro can destroy anyone overnight."

Prime Minister Castro did in fact politically assassinate his own chosen President, Manuel Urrutia, in a four-hour television speech, with Urrutia resigning his office and fleeing the Presidential Palace minutes after Castro had completed his broadcast.

Castro's charges against Urrutia: One, he had bought a $40,000 home; two, he had publicly attacked the Communists, while Castro's policy has been one of neutrality; and three, he had been slow in signing into law some of the revolutionary decrees. These offenses, Castro said, amounted to "near treason."

Anti-U. S. Feeling

Dr. Castro asked the public to indicate whether Urrutia should stay or resign. When crowds formed in front of the President's Palace, Urrutia and his family fled. Dr. Castro said this action was democracy in action, "the purest since ancient Greece."

On the part of the average citizen, one finds sur-

prisingly little anti-American feeling, despite Fidel Castro's almost daily attacks on the United States.

But among the hard-core of the revolutionaries, the feeling against the U.S. is intense. We are blamed for a too – friendly attitude toward the Batista regime, and for having acted improperly as far back as 1898.

Apple Blossom Festival

✳✳✳✳

The Shenandoah Apple Blossom Festival became a tradition in Winchester in 1924. The Festival will celebrate its 80th anniversary in 2007. The event has been held annually, except during World War II (1942-45).

As a 9-year-old, I had the role of page, riding on the Queen's float, and have attended every festival since, with the exception of my first two years at college, at the Virginia Military Institute.

Two Presidents of the United States have participated in the festival – Lyndon Johnson and Gerald Ford. Each crowned his daughter as Queen Shenandoah.

I have participated in one form or another in about half of them, serving as both Grand Marshal of the Grand Feature Parade and the same year, 1980, as Minister of the Crown.

I have been vice president of the organization for 45 years, and was the official escort for 34 Apple Blossom Festival queens, having selected quite a number, including the 1937 queen, Gretchen Thomson of New Orleans. In 1941, I persuaded Gretchen to marry me.

Mrs. Byrd and I, over a 20-year period, hosted 20 festival queens at our home.

Luci Baines Johnson, the 1964 Queen Shenandoah, stayed at our home and at breakfast told me "she was mad at her father because he was not coming to Winchester to crown her as queen."

Later that morning, when I went to The Winchester Star, of which I was editor and publisher, I told the managing editor, Jack Davis, that the President *would* be here to crown his daughter queen. Jack said he had already called the White House and they told him the President *was not* coming to Winchester. I told Jack that he *was*.

Two hours later, Jack called the White House again and was told that the President *would not* be here. I told the managing editor again that the President would be here and to be prepared, if necessary, to hold the press 10-15 minutes beyond deadline (The Star was an afternoon paper then.)

The President arrived by helicopter seven minutes prior to the crowning ceremony.

When the managing editor asked how I could be so certain the president would be here when the White House said he would not, I replied, "It was easy. His daughter told me at breakfast that she was mad with him because he had attended the crowning of her older sister as queen of the Azalea Festival in Norfolk. So, I felt certain that no father would show such favoritism."

I have been a strong supporter of the festival all

through the years.

The festival is a year-round operation, requiring a small paid staff. But hundreds of local volunteers are the backbone of the annual event.

What I like best is the fact that the festival brings the entire community together, with everyone working for a common cause. It is truly a local event.

Leadership Awards

※※※※

In 1994, I established an endowment at the University of Virginia to award outstanding high school students, one from each of the state's 11 congressional districts. I did it by congressional districts, otherwise the bulk of awards likely would go to areas with the greatest resources, namely Northern Virginia.

I created this program because of my deep conviction that a strong system of public education is essential to democratic government, and that cultivating leadership among young citizens advances both education and government.

The program is similar to one I started in 1954 at The Winchester Star, of which I was publisher; the next year I established a similar program for the Daily News-Record in Harrisonburg.

Each September, the president of the University of Virginia writes the principal of every high school in Virginia, inviting the nomination of a graduating senior who best demonstrates a combination of academic accomplishment, excellence of character, qualities of leadership, and devotion to duty.

The approximately 300 nominations each year are then reviewed by a committee of deans of admission from five Virginia colleges. That committee culls the list to 33, three from each of the 11 congressional districts.

These 33 students are then interviewed by a committee of nine under the chairmanship of former Chief Justice of the Virginia Supreme Court, Harry L. Carrico. It includes the presidents of two Virginia colleges and business leaders. From three nominees of the 11 congressional districts, the committee chooses one to receive a $10,000 award. There is no restriction on the use of the award.

I established this award with the hope it would accomplish the following:

- Focus increased attention on the importance of education;
- Create a desire for excellence among students;
- Enhance student self-assurance by the Selection Committee's vote of confidence; and
- Provide recognition and financial assistance to students with outstanding leadership qualities.

Clinton Impeachment

✷✷✷✷

In September 1998, President William Jefferson Clinton was impeached, namely indicted, by the House of Representatives for the felony charge of perjury.

The indictment of President Clinton was sent to the U.S. Senate for either acquittal or conviction. If convicted, the constitution provides only one punishment – removal from office. It requires a two-third vote, namely 67 senators to convict.

Not being in the Congress at that time – I retired from the Senate in 1983 – I, of course, could not vote on the issue. I had voted against electing Mr. Clinton in each of his two campaigns.

But many persons have asked how I would have voted had I been at that time in the Congress. Most, especially my two sons, have been amazed with my reply. I thought I would use this occasion to make it known.

First, had I been in the House of Representatives, I would have voted to impeach. President Clinton clearly violated his office by committing a felony – namely perjury, lying under oath to the Congress and to the American people. I thought he deserved punishment. I would have voted to impeach.

Had I been a member of the Senate, I would have

faced a different problem. The constitution provides only one punishment for a presidential indictment – removal from office.

President Clinton clearly committed perjury. While the offense was obviously indictable, it was totally personal in nature.

So I reasoned with myself as one who voted against him in each of his two elections, and at which point he received the votes of more than 50 million Americans.

I argued with myself: Could I justify removing him from office by votes of 67 senators versus the action of more than 50 million voters who elected him?

It could be justified, yes. But I could not bring myself to believe that the crime justified removal from office to which he had been elected by popular vote.

I would have voted, as did the majority of the senators, against removal. In my judgment, the punishment did not fit the crime.

Secret Service Protection

✳✳✳✳

In the 1950s I was a guest of the editor of the Kansas City Star at the Gridiron Club's annual dinner. The Gridiron Club's membership (about 60) is confined to the Washington correspondents of newspapers from throughout the United States.

While small in numbers, Gridiron has 600 guests at its annual dinners. The list includes the President and Vice President of the United States, several members of the Supreme Court, about half of the President's Cabinet, top military leaders, a few members of the Senate and top business leaders from throughout the nation.

Off the banquet room is a long room to which special guests are invited. My host asked me to be there early, which I was. The door was open, so I walked in and saw an individual at the other end of the room. He was alone. He began walking toward me. I did the same toward him and quickly realized who it was. When he got close enough to shake hands, he identified himself as Dwight Eisenhower. No Secret Service in sight.

I include this vignette for two reasons:

First, it tells me a lot about a great American. Not as a president. Not as a general. But as an individual –

Dwight David Eisenhower.

Secondly, it dramatizes the huge difference in how presidents now are protected. When I attended last year's Gridiron dinner, Secret Service were everywhere, and one could not get anywhere near the special guest room.

New York Ticker-Tape Parade - 1926

50th Anniversary Trip To Antarctica - 1979

✳✳✳✳

In 1926 as an 11-year-old, I had an amazing experience.

Richard E. Byrd, my father's younger brother, became the first person to fly an airplane over the North Pole. Aviation was in its infancy. For that feat, he received the Congressional Medal of Honor.

The City of New York honored him with a parade through the streets of America's largest city. The admiral, of course, was in the lead car for what was known as the "ticker-tape parade," getting its name from the fact that tons of paper were shredded into confetti and thrown from the business houses and residences along the parade route.

My father was governor of Virginia at that time. I rode in the parade in the car with him and my grandmother.

I was fascinated by the masses of cheering New Yorkers who not only lined the sidewalks but also were throwing what looked like a blizzard of ticker tape from the windows of the tall buildings lining the parade route.

It was indeed an event no 11-year-old boy could ever forget.

I had a somewhat similar experience 53 years later when, as a U. S. senator, I was asked by the government to go to Antarctica to honor the 50th anniversary of Admiral Byrd's historic flight over the South Pole. That event was organized by the National Science Foundation in November 1979.

I flew from Washington to New Zealand and then to McMurdo Station in Antarctica. McMurdo was America's base for scientific studies.

Antarctica is an uninhabited continent, larger than the United States. It is totally white. The continent is snow and ice-packed over the centuries, nearly two miles deep.

About 15 countries have small bases for scientific purposes scattered on the shores of that vast expanse. Indeed, throughout that huge continent, there are no living creatures except penguins and seals near the ocean shores. And beyond a 50-mile distance from the ocean there are no living creatures on that continent.

Antarctica is in total darkness for six months and total light the other six months. Once darkness sets in, the crevasses are too many and too dangerous to permit travel by either dog sled or even the landing of an airplane.

November is the first month of light. The 1979 party of 15 scientists to which I was attached flew by Navy plane to the South Pole, taking off from McMurdo on wheels, and landing at the South Pole on skis.

There was a small outpost there; 21 American scientists – 20 men and a woman doctor – had "wintered over," having been there during the period of total darkness, living in quonset hut-type buildings.

Antarctica is considered an ideal place to conduct weather studies. One of the purposes of Admiral Byrd returning three years after his flight was to live under the ice during the six months of darkness, conducting scientific studies.

November 27, 1979 Senator Byrd and Dr. Laurence Gould leaving Christchurch, New Zealand for Antarctica, hoping to arrive November 29 at the South Pole, the 50th anniversary of Admiral Richard Byrd's historic flight over the pole in 1929. Senator Byrd is the Admiral's nephew and Dr. Gould was second in command of the 1929 expedition.

We had a small ceremony at the South Pole suitable for a 50th anniversary.

On that day in 1979, all of us did something Admiral Byrd could not do. He had circled the pole, but his airplane could not carry enough fuel to permit a landing.

We, many years later, were able to stand where he could not.

His 1929 take-off from Little America, which he named his base, was without incident. But about midway through his 700-mile flight, he found a mountain range higher than had been expected. To get across the mountain, he had to lighten the plane. This he did by throwing overboard all the emergency food and equipment the plane was carrying.

For us, it was a fascinating trip. I appreciated all the more the dangers endured by Antarctic explorers.

A Project I Cherish -
Annie Bronson Foundation

****

All sorts of strange things happen when one is representing 5 million people. Some are a bit bizarre.

But one I feel an especially deep obligaton to, and still cherish, even after a third of a century has gone by.

Several years after becoming a U.S. Senator, I began getting mail from Annie Bronson who identified herself as the secretary of a professor at Harvard University. She said she had been reading my speeches and liked my philosophy.

I gave prompt response, either the same day or the following day, as promptness in answering mail was a requirement in my office.

So, Annie Bronson and I became pen pals. She would write me four or five times a year about my speeches or pending legislation, or my views on matters of interest to her.

That went on for seven or eight years, when I received a letter asking: "Would you mind at my death if I left you my entire estate to be used for the benefit of the United States?"

The document specified that I was accountable to no one. It was mine to be handled as I wished. She added that her employer urged her to leave it to Harvard, but, she wrote, "I trust you more than I trust Harvard."

I was not only deeply touched but also felt greatly honored and under obligation to handle with care her life's savings.

I formed the Annie Bronson Charitable Foundation with her professor, her lawyer and myself as trustees. Now, with the other two no longer around, I assigned my two sons to assume that reponsibility.

I find it a difficult task to determine how to use the income from the $300,000-$500,000 endowment for the benefit of the United States.

I never met nor even saw Annie Bronson, but from her letters, and a few telephone conversations, I feel I can rather accurately guess what might appeal to her.

Contributions have been made to:

- U.S. Capitol Historical Society
- Lincoln Family Cemetery,
  Rockingham County, Va.
- Citizens for Sound Economy
- George Washington Office Museum,
  Winchester, Va.
- Henry & Williams Evans Home for Children,
  Winchester, Va.
- Society of the Cincinnati

- Scholarships
- National D-Day Memorial, Bedford, Va.
- Mount Vernon Ladies Association

I am assuming the United States is benefiting by her funds by helping young people get an education or the Lincoln Family Cemetery because her father was in Lincoln's Army during the Civil War. As Ms. Bronson was very patriotic, I thought non-profit charities and patriotic groups would be fitting recipients of her estate.

Washington Dinners

✳✳✳✳

There is a great deal of social life in Washington, D. C. Mrs. Byrd and I, however, held it to a minimum.

I found my work in the Senate too demanding, especially since I spent two to four nights a week making speeches or meeting with constituents somewhere in Virginia.

There were only two dinners I always attended. One is the **Alfalfa Club**. The **Alfalfa Club** is a non-partisan social organization in Washington, founded in 1913. The name Alfalfa was chosen to honor **Medicago sativa**, the plant that sends its roots deepest in search of liquid refreshment.

The short answer to what the Alfalfa Club does is "Not much." Its main object is to make life brighter for its members and their friends. Speeches are political and always in good humor and never in bad taste.

Beginning in 1945, every President of the United States except two – Clinton and Carter – have been members. I was voted a member in 1948 and have attended annually since that date.

Its membership of 150 is nationwide – business leaders and professionals from throughout the nation, generals and admirals, newspaper publishers, and about

20 senators.

For example, at the January 2007 dinner, the following were inducted into membership of the Alfalfa Club:

Michael M. Bloomberg, Mayor, New York City;
Elaine L. Chao, Secretary of Labor;
Susan M. Collins, Republican senator, Maine;
Michael Dell, CEO, Dell, Inc.;
Jane Harman, Democratic congresswoman, California;
Mark S. Pryor, Democratic senator, Arkansas;
John G. Roberts, Jr., The Chief Justice of the United States.

The President of the United States ends the dinner with a short humorous speech.

I attended my first Alfalfa Club dinner as the guest of my father in 1936 and for the next 12 years. I was elected a member in 1948. Having attended each dinner since 1936, in 2006 I attended my 66th dinner. None was held during four war years.

Incidentally, Lyndon Johnson was president of the **Alfalfa Club** when fate made him President of the United States (he kept his membership in **Alfalfa** but resigned its presidency).

Another club I attend annually, not as a member but as a guest, is the famed **Gridiron Club**. The membership of this club is confined to the Washington correspondents of newspapers from throughout the United States. I have attended more than 50 Gridiron dinners – more than any living person.

So with these two organizations, I continue my close association with both politics and newspapers, the same double trouble.

MEMBERSHIPS

- National Conference of Editorial Writers (since 1947)
- Rotary (since 1935)
- National Press Club (since 1938)
- Army-Navy Club, Washington, DC (since 1942)
- Alfalfa Club, Washington, DC (since 1948)
- Commonwealth Club, Richmond, VA (since 1948)
- Benevolent & Protective Order of Elks (since 1937)
- Winchester Country Club (since 1935)
- Veterans of Foreign Wars
- American Legion
- 15 years as a director and then Vice President, Associated Press, 1950 - 1965.
- Director, Park Communications
- Director, O'Sullivan Corporation
- Trustee, Shenandoah University
- Advisor, Tax Foundation
- 33 degree Mason & Honorary Inspector General Masonic Order
- Trustee and Honorary Vice President Virginia Historical Society.
- Rockingham Publishing Company, since 1937
- Winchester Evening Star, since 1935